MORAL EDUCATION

Historical Perspectives

Larry C. Jensen
Richard S. Knight

UNIVERSITY
PRESS OF
AMERICA

LANHAM • NEW YORK • LONDON

Copyright © 1981 by

University Press of America,™ Inc.

4720 Boston Way
Lanham, MD 20706

3 Henrietta Street
London WC2E 8LU England

Library of Congress Cataloging in Publication Data

Jensen, Larry C.
    Moral education.

    Bibliography: p.
    1. Moral education—History. I. Knight,
Richard S. II. Title
LC268.J43   370.11'4'09   80-5896
ISBN 0-8191-1919-9   AACR2
ISBN 0-8191-1920-2 (pbk.)

Dedication

This book is dedicated to our daughters, Kim and Jane.

Acknowledgements

We wish to acknowledge the valuable library research and help on the first draft given by Scott Couch. We also appreciate the patient and skillful typing by Vicki Castner.

CONTENTS

PREFACE

With few exceptions, societies from the time
of Aristotle have accepted two fundamental beliefs.
The first is that mankind should be moral and the
second is that morality can be taught and learned.
The unanswered questions are: What is morality?
And, how is it developed? Social institutions,
such as the family, church, schools and government have had different answers for the above
questions. But the striking element is that they
have always had answers. For the Greeks, virtues
were few and simple, such as wisdom, courage, and
temperance. The virtues were to be taught to those
who would be rulers. To the medieval Christians,
virtues were associated with the tenants of the
Christian church and were to be inculcated in the
youth. However, in our contemporary urban and
rapidly changing society, it is difficult to know
who is teaching morality and what morality is being
taught. This is particularly noticeable in the
United States where there has been an open and formal separation of church and state. During past
centuries, virtue and morality came directly from
religion. Now, in the United States, the civil
government, in order to avoid denominational partiality, has carefully restrained itself from formally
teaching and prescribing moral values, except the
most obvious elements which are reflected in the law.
The religious institutions, on the other hand, have
not been adequate to teach morality on a national
level because they not only lack power and sanctions,
but no one church includes a majority of the population in the heterogeneous society.

Nevertheless, the church, government, family,
and school have emerged as the major institutions
which prescribe and teach morality. To propose
that one of these institutions has exclusive responsibility in this area seems foolish, as all evidence
suggests that each institution will continue to
exist and function as a socializing agency. The

ix

church will continue to teach morality, for religion and morality have become intertwined during the past centuries; the family, entrusted with the socialization of children, must inevitably deal with the most basic issues of moral behavior when rearing children; the government in establishing and maintaining civil and criminal law must both advocate and educate the citizenry with respect to law. Of the four main institutions mentioned, only the school's role in educating morality is held in question.

When the school is regarded as an extention or an arm of a religion then the answer is clear; it must serve the needs of the church, and hence moral education is mandatory. When the school is regarded as the arm or extension of civil government, its commitment to education in the area of civil and criminal law cannot legally be questioned because the school is regarded as an extension of government. In communistic states, schools teach the values of communism or advocate communism while attacking democracy and other forms of government; the converse is true in a democracy. Certainly citizenship, respect for the flag, obedience to local, state, and federal law are openly taught in United States public schools. Values, attitudes, and virtues associated with democracy are advocated; for example, the dignity of each individual, respect for life, the right to private property, and the need for citizen participation in government can be openly taught. However, when the schools have extended their curriculum to include aspects of morality related to or closely tied with religion, the courts have viewed it unfavorably. The most direct limitation imposed by the courts has been against public prayers in public schools.

In general, it is unclear what aspects of morality public schools may include and what aspects of morality must remain with the family and religion. To make matters more complex for educators, about 33% of parents surveyed in 1981 wanted moral principles taught in schools and "discipline problems" with their moral overtones are consistently

rated as the most serious problem facing public
schools.

In order to better understand the role of
moral and character education in the public schools,
an historical overview is needed, and thus, this
book was written.

CHAPTER I

UNDERSTANDING MORAL PERSPECTIVES

A Trobriander Cannibal was told that a great war was continuing in Europe, and that after one battle, the number of men killed was so great that it would be possible to entirely cover the island where the Trobrianderler lived. The Trobrianderler looked at the European in disbelief, and said that it was impossible to eat so much flesh. After the European explained that there were no cannibals in Europe where this battle took place, the Trobrianderler was even further perplexed and dismayed, exclaiming, "It is a shame to kill so many people for no use."[1]

This dialogue between the European and the cannibal is not an argument for cultural relativism, but rather an illustration of difference of perspective possible between two individuals observing the same event, and the even greater difference in their interpretation. It is felt that an appreciation of differences in moral reasoning between social cultures, eras, and even individuals within a culture, is a desirable prerequisite for understanding the material in subsequent chapters. All stable societies have rules which are upheld by a system of justice usually based on some type of sanction system, with rewards and penalties. In more advanced societies, these rules are codified and have an elaborate system of enforcement; in more primitive societies the operation of informal rules is frequently difficult to identify and interpret.

A unique combination of influences determine any individual's socialization pattern and system of values. These patterns vary greatly within one society and even more between dissimilar societies. However, nearly everyone agrees that it is important to help children in any society move in the direction of a more mature set of values and beliefs and to behave in accordance with at least some standard of behavior.

1

Sometimes variations in socialization patterns are due to situational value systems or to the importance attached to different virtues. In war, military virtues of courage and discipline may dominate; in affluent times, a scientific spirit may be encouraged and value is placed upon virtues associated with leisure activities. Functionalism is a term applied to a school of thought that implies that cultural practices, beliefs, and patterns develop primarily as they are useful to the existence of the society. Different types of marriages may occur and different types of sexual activities may be permitted depending upon the extent to which they foster or promote the well being of the society. Basically, the argument of the functionalist is reduced to different ways of meeting primary needs. For example, it has been suggested that checks on early sex relations unconsciously aim at prolonging the period of youth when (especially in more advanced societies) a longer period of socialization is required.

Then there are differences due to the type and extent of moral insight and reasoning. Tribesmen who eat their parents combine the rule that mankind should honor his parents and also acquire virtues. They believe that the attributes of a person whom they eat will become their own. If this dietary fallacy were true, it would be hard to deny that this was not the highest form of honoring ones' parents.

Some examples have been presented to support the premise that morality depends upon one's culture. One source of this variability is due to the difference in the importance given the same act in different social situations. A second is due to variations arising from changes in knowledge or belief regarding the normal qualities of acts and their consequences. That variations in moral judgments arise from the amount of knowledge available in the culture is apparent when we consider the treatment of the insane, who in previous years were tortured and burned with the intent of forcing them to reveal that they were actually witches, or possessed of evil spirits.

2

Because functionalists believe that moral beliefs and actions meet primary needs, there will invariably be a variation in the importance given to different virtues when conditions affecting need satisfaction vary. Factors influencing moral beliefs include the physical environment, type of economy, philosophy and religion, social class, and urban/rural differences. While not all-inclusive, these factors are considered to be the most salient and are presented to help the reader appreciate the complexity of forces that influence moral behavior.

Physical Environment

Perhaps the first man to note the long term effects of the physical environment on human behavior was Aristotle, who believed that those who live in a cold climate as in Europe are full of spirit, but wanting intelligence and skill; therefore, they retain comparative freedom but have no political organization and are incapable of ruling over others. On the other hand, the natives of Asia are intelligent and inventive, but wanting in spirit, and therefore are always in a state of subjection and slavery. But the Hellenic race, situated between them is intermediate in character, being high spirited and also intelligent.

While history would present numerous problems for Aristotle, later cultural anthropologists have espoused similar notions sometimes with the same ethnocentric bias. A long observation of history shows that farming and herding are the forerunners of civilization whereas hunting, fishing, and other types of nomadic-type life do not result in a concrete base upon which to erect a civilization. Others have argued that the subsistance economies without a surplus of food result in a more ready acceptance of cultural rules and tradition which are necessary to maintain a surplus and to produce the substance of life for years to come. Individual deviation jeopardizes the social well being and a premium is placed on obedience to the older and wiser elders of the community and upon responsibility to those tasks assigned to the faithful member.

3

The type of morality and reasoning which would develop in a hunting and fishing culture would be markedly different from an agrarian society. Individualistic and aggressive behavior is more probable in a hunting or fishing culture where individual skill is at a premium, and initiative or innovation will not have a serious detrimental effect if it fails and may frequently bring about immediate positive results. The research team of Berry, Child, and Bacon, have found that this general premise did hold up and concluded that pressure towards obedience and a general value on responsibility are higher in high food accumulation economies whose food supply must be stored to protect life throughout the year.[2] Values focusing on self reliance and achievement are more common in societies with low accumulation of food.

Unfortunately, controlled experiments or even field observations which test the influence of physical environment on values or moral behavior are rare. While history is replete with examples of people changing as a result of movement from one climate to another, it has been impossible to assess the extent to which associated moral changes are due to the new physical surroundings or to other factors associated with change of residence. This same objection may be raised when comparing people of one geographic location with another.

Economic

In entrepreneurial occupations such as medicine, small business, door-to-door selling or contract fruit picking, the individual must rely upon required skills, self reliance, and hard work to obtain success. In bureaucratic occupations, on the contrary, job security is high and success usually implies conformity and adjustment to the group norms. When studied, these two groups of people have different attitudes about the world and the attitudes and behaviors they desire for their children. Entrepreneurials as a group are harsher in their child rearing and expect more initiative and self reliance from

4

their child. They are stricter in delineation of sex roles, and more traditional in their family morality.[3] Eric Fromm in his popular book, The Sane Society, illustrates how man can become more conforming and dependent on others as economic situations change towards more social and economic interdependence.[4]

Social Class

McCandless in a textbook, Children, Behavior and Development, describes thirteen values which separate the middle class from the lower lower class.[5] He points out and generally documents that lower class children belong to different church groups and also practice a more fundamental type of religion. They place less value on cleanliness, savings, and reason. Lower class children are said to be more physically aggressive and sexually promiscuous, although the word promiscuous implies a value judgment. Middle class parents are more likely to espouse nonprofanity, honesty, the protestant work ethic, and responsibility and the value of learning.

Numerous reasons can be cited to explain these differences such as the lack of facilities for cleanliness, the inability to earn enough money, difficulties on saving the rewards from hard work, living conditions that directly affect sexual behavior, education that affects language, and social acceptance. Surveys of child rearing practices frequently point out differences between social classes in the terms of behavioral goals, concepts of morality, and acceptable behavior. A research analysis of the new morality has found social class differences in the American youth of the 1970's.[6] Frequently, the differences attributed to races or minority groups are actually due to social class differences which are confounded in the research designs.

Philosophy and Religion

It is common to equate morals and religion. However, in other eras religion was divorced from

5

morality. Philosophy has entered and left its marriage with moral behavior periodically throughout the ages. At the present time, philosophy has moved away and currently is not closely associated with morality, but conventional 20th century religion is closely intertwined. Men's early polytheistic gods were not necessarily moral; the association of morality with God developed as man became monotheistic. In an interesting study addressed to this problem, researchers compared beliefs between cultures believing in gods that were either malevolent or benevolent.[7] Their data indicated that aggressive, supernatural gods tended to occur in societies where parents rewarded self reliance and independence, and valued punishment as a means of controlling behavior. Since the research was of a correlational nature, it is impossible to determine if the belief in gods caused the belief in the values or if certain values held in that culture influenced the personal attributes the people assigned to the god. Nevertheless, data strongly suggests there is a relationship between the two.

Politics and Law

It is usually held that the influence of morality on law is more pronounced than the converse. However, the effect of one upon the other is worth noting. Politicians frequently state that you can't legislate morality but the influence of court-ordered desegregation in schooling, housing, and business has made an obvious impact on behavior of the white and black communities in the United States. It might be noted that governments change in basic values, beliefs, and behavior. The most dramatic and widespread demonstration of the effects of politics on morality occurred in the Soviet Union when they abruptly changed from monarchy to communism. Under communism, a number of unplanned experiments occurred in terms of enacting legislation toward the family, expecially the role of the family in child rearing, and divorce. In Russia earlier in this century, comparative laxness was placed on sexual behavior and a great deal of what would commonly be called promiscuous behavior occurred as well as quickly-obtained divorces.

Then there was abrupt change in official policy. Each time legislation was enacted, there was a corresponding change in the behavior of the citizenry. The completeness and thoroughness with which moral behavior has been legislated in the Soviet Union is due to the unity between morality and political belief. Speaking of an autonomous morality (not officially recognized in Soviet theory), Richard T. Degeorge in Soviet Ethics in Morality states that to recognize it as a desirable morality, however, would be to lay the party open to external moral scrutiny.[8] It would admit fallability, and the possiblity of other human values. Degeorge also states that the Soviet claim of coincidence between morality which is taught and that which is practiced is, in fact, not true. However, even to claim coincidence indicates that there is a much closer correspondence in the Soviet Union than in most Western cultures. The Soviet Union perhaps more than any other country outside of China has effectively worked to develop the program of moral education or inculcation which has been described by Urie Bronfenbrenner in Soviet Methods of Character Education.[9] The main goal of Soviet moral education is to bring the individual into compliance with the collective.

It is extremely interesting to note that the differences in philosophy between the U.S.S.R. and the nation of Israel result in quite different behaviors and programs for the respective countries, even though each tries to develop the individual for a collective or communal-type living. Perhaps political theory differing in the role and importance of the individual is responsible for the fact that striking differences occur between the kibbutz and the U.S.S.R. school. In the kibbutz, there is very limited competition, whereas a highly competitive program is introduced and maintained in the Soviet school. Individuality is encouraged in the kibbutz, whereas, compliance and conformity to the state is central in the Communist program.

7

Socialization Goals

The listing of factors which influence moral
behavior is not meant to be exhaustive and obviously no single factor exerts its effect in isolation. The combined effects of these factors is
apparent as we contrast the morality found in primitive cultures with that of modern urban industrialized society. In a primitive culture without
written codified laws and with non-virtuous gods,
a stranger in their midst may be without law. His
fate is often cruel and no moral or ethical compunc-
tion is stirred in the members of the primitive
group inasmuch as he is a stranger and outside the
rule of both morals and law. However, property
rights, rights of individuals and personal rights of
integrity within the primitive culture are probably
more carefully guarded and maintained than in an
impersonal society characterized by the urban ethics.

One does not even have to look as far back as
primitive society to find a comparison with our
modern society that illustrates how factors unite
to form different patterns of morality, values and
beliefs. Robert Sundly, in reviewing early 19th
century American literature on child rearing, noted
that at that time the major Orthodox Christian point
of view was that man is deprived and damned through
original sin. From this point of view, a child's
will needs to be broken so the child could submit to
God's will. Here is an episode reported by Sundly:

> One mother writing in the mother's
> magazine in 1834 described how her 16-
> month-old girl refused to say "dear
> mama" upon the father's order. She was
> led into a room alone where she screamed
> wildly for 10 minutes then she was com-
> manded again and again refused. She was
> then whipped and asked again. This kept
> up for four hours until the child finally
> obeyed.[10]

The comparison of this advice with that of the
20th century spokesman Dr. Spock is obvious. It is

8

interesting to reflect about values that have produced various ethics or values common to different
eras. For example, the 14th century gentleman was
noble as a result of birth. But by the time of
Thomas Smith during the 16th century, new conditions
were asserting themselves. The most obvious was the
degredation of manual work. A gentleman was expected
to be a man of leisure not of work. Compare such an
ethic with that of Benjamin Franklin who espoused
what is usually called the Protestant Ethic. In this
ethic, hard work, self sacrifice and thrift were
espoused, leading to a leisure-free, hard-driving,
and independent individual acting in whatever way he
could to accumulate the virtues and profits of work.

While it is difficult to specify the prevailing
ethic of the 20th century, because values are changing so quickly, the reader has probably concluded that
pleasurelessness, hard work, self denial, and thrift
are not included as major virtues. These diversities
in thought and action may now help clarify consider-
ations of what is moral thought and behavior.

Defining Morality

The reader may have asked for a definition of
morality but a consideration of the preceeding factors
or effects were felt to be necessary before resolving
some kind of resolution to the question of "What is
moral?" One possible answer is to define moral as a
choice of action in terms of what is considered right
or wrong. It is hoped that the value of this tentative definition will become evident as we discuss
moral action and moral thought in subsequent chapters.

It is proposed that a definition of morality may
best be made in a social context. While the reader
is asked to arrive at his own decision, it seems ad-
visable to establish a guiding set of principles which
are reasonably compatible and incorporate some of the
discussed elements. This should still allow for com-
parable freedom of thought, action, and individuality.
Assuming that one has framed a set of values, one must

then learn to relate them with others in a societal context. He shares his values with whom he interacts.

Before proceeding to more specific influences on moral behavior, it may be well to consider a concept taught to the senior author by G. Stanley Ratner of Michigan State University. Professor Ratner pointed out that many of our beliefs, preferences, and decisions are not based on a rational analysis, but rather largely dependent on unconscious philosophical assumptions or beliefs. It is the authors' contention that most readers will likely believe, practice, and perhaps even understand only that information which is congruent with their unconscious assumptions. For example, most readers will lean towards one of the three basic philosophical positions about the basic nature of a human being. The first, strongly stated by early Christian theologians, is the doctrine of original sin or infant depravity. This theme has been dominant in Western society resulting in a parental belief that the young child is both evil and rebellious. Since the child's basic nature was antisocial, the job of the parent was to suppress or curb the basic nature of the child that he might become a civilized person and return to God. Obviously, the social institutions were considered assets to the parent.

In opposition to this point of view, men such as Jean Jacques Rousseau believed that natural man, i.e., man before his corruption by social institutions is basically good. It is society that produces evil in man. He believed, as espoused in his book, Emile, that the child would naturally move in the direction of goodness and purity, but that contact and influence received from parents, church, and other institutions of society brought corruption to the pure and innocent child. The reader has perhaps heard the analogy that the child is like a flower and given the basic essentials of life will unfold and gradually blossom into beautiful and moral maturity.

10

A third view, usually traced back at least as far as John Locke, held that the child is a tabula rasa; the child is considered a blank slate upon which can be written either good or bad and that he has the complete potential for either, being infinitely malleable. If unconscious beliefs about this basic nature of man influence choices, then psychological theory should reflect these elementary philosophical bases. An examination of current psychological theories indicates that these do occur. The traditional Freudian theory postulates that man's basic energy originates from two basic instincts (life and death) which when translated become sex and aggression, and in Freud's victorian culture these had a definite anti-social, negative connotation.

Contemporary phenomenological psychologists such as Carl Rogers, Abraham Maslow, and others point out that the individual has a basic, natural, inner growth drive towards morality.[11] If the individual is provided with only the minimal essentials for physical and psychological growth, he will move forward as a fully functioning person. Unfortunately, the environments into which a child is born are distorted, perverse, and in other ways not conducive or supporting of the inner growth drive. Such children become psychologically and morally malformed. When these persons seek professional help, the psychologist tries to create a psychological climate especially conducive or promoting of personal growth. The basic morals, a desired ethical outlook, can be expected to naturally emerge in this facilitating environment. The reader may see the similarity to Rousseau's unfolding flower.

Modern-day behaviorists emphasize the malleability of character. The individual is assumed to be capable of a wide range or moral behavior, and the particular act he displays in any moral situation is determined by his past learning. Often the words, learning and conditioning, are used synonymously. Thus, this psychological theory basically rests on assumptions very similar to Locke's "Tabula Rasa",

11

the Freudian theory is similar to the Calvanistic natural badness of man and the phenomenologists restate Rousseau's noble natural man concept. Other psychological theories probably are influenced by basic philosophical presupposition; at least individual preference for psychological theory is partially determined by unconscious philosophical beliefs.

Now, after presenting information about the diversity in moral beliefs and practices, the basic nature of man, and considering how it is likely that preferences for psychological theory are differentially influenced, the question of what is moral behavior is still unresolved! It is proposed that the goals of socialization for an individual are influenced by a combination of the preceeding factors. It seems unlikely to the authors that many readers will be in very close agreement at this time. However, most readers may agree that it is important to help children move into the direction of a more mature set of values and beliefs and to behave in accordance with at least some standard of behavior.

CHAPTER II

A COMPARISON BETWEEN A PRIMITIVE
SOCIETY AND MODERN AMERICA

Moral education in primitive societies is usually much easier for the children and youth than our more conscious moral and values education in modern times. Perhaps the main difference stems from the fact that primitive societies are small, homogeneous and integrated. Children can readily observe the correct way to behave by simply watching adults and older children. The adults model the proper behavior and the children imitate it.

Children in a modern culture can't easily imitate adults. They are exposed to too many adults whose dress, language, life style and specific moral behavior vary greatly. Upper middle class Episcopalian parents who live in Boston don't want their children to imitate low class non-religious unemployed adults. Most parents are apprehensive about homosexual school teachers because they fear the teacher may serve as a model of an acceptable adult life style.

Pluralism as found in large cities in the United States has many positive values. But pluralism does not provide a coherent moral model for the young to imitate. Children must make very subtle discriminations about who is an acceptable adult model and who is not. Furthermore, most children can't help their fathers at work or even observe what they do. Children in primitive societies can watch their fathers and often help much as children on farms nowadays can. The child in advanced societies can't observe or help their mothers as much either as increasing numbers of mothers work away from home at paying jobs (over 50% of women in 1979.)[1] Adolescents and children in the U.S. have peers, television characters and teachers as models available to them for at least as much time as their parents.

13

Another reason why becoming socialized and developing a coherent system of values is difficult for the modern child is that religion is usually separated from the routine of life. Although 95% of population of the U.S. profess a belief in god,[2] less than 50% attend church regularly. In contrast, everyone in a Bushman village on the Kalahari Desert in Africa participates in the dances, religious ceremonies and is blessed by the medicine man.[3]

In primitive societies, because they are small, everyone participates and one can become a leader by growing older.

In order to give the reader some specific examples of the differences in moral education in a modern industrialized literate society such as the U.S. and a primitive pre-literate hunting and gathering society, a comparision will be made between the ! Kung Bushmen who inhabit the Dobi area of the Kalahari Desert in Botswana.

First, it may be useful to remind ourselves of how moral education is carried on in the U.S. in the 1980's. In spite of rapid secularization, religion still appears to be the basis of much of morality. About half of the population attend church and would receive formal religious instruction to some degree. But many adults and young people receive their values which have their basis in religion through their families without being very active in a formal church. For example, it is common for children to rebel and stop attending church services when they become adolescents. However, early training and traditional family values have been thoroughly inculcated by teen years for most individuals. Although changing, the Protestant Ethic and conservative values still seem to be esteemed as evidenced by a series of Gallup polls[4] and by the conservative tide in the 1980 presidential and congressional election outcomes. In addition, Boy and Girl Scouts, 4-H, and other voluntary youth groups have traditional values and morality within their ideals.[5]

14

Morality in modern America is transmitted in many ways. As in traditional societies, children imitate their parents and attractive adults. As mentioned above, children in developed societies must make fine discriminations about which adults and other children are appropriate models. In addition to imitating appropriate models, modern children and youth are exposed to considerable systematic exhortation and subtle morality inculcation. If children are church goers they will hear stories from scriptures, hear sermons, and receive encouragement and admonishment from ministers, teachers and friendly, concerned adults in the congregation.

Parochial schools and other private schools usually make values and morality education a regular part of the curriculum. Public schools are legally obliged to remain secular and maintain a clear distinction between church and state.

Nevertheless, public schools have a clear mandate and a "hidden curriculum" to encourage punctuality and regular attendance, to encourage children to be respectful of adults and those in authority, and to be polite and tactful. These values are especially important to teachers! Schools also stress helping others (except on tests), a sense of accomplishment, and intellectual skills such as reading and writing.

Schools give mixed messages to students about competition, cooperation and winning. Virtually every student knows it is good to be a winner, especially in male athletics. In fact, winning in athletics or getting good grades in some schools is more esteemed than honesty. So some adolescents come to think that winning justifies some forms of cheating. Later in professional sports and business the same value conflict persists and morality is confused for many youth and young adults.

Although on the surface most Americans subscribe to the value of equality, the commitment is usually to an abstract ideal. In practice, America is an open class society but not a classless society. Morality for the low class is different from the upper class. This is clearly apparent in the federally ordered attempts at integration by busing controversy that continues to surround schools. Experts such as James Coleman maintain that race is a peripheral issue in school busing. Social class is what matters. When lower class children are integrated with middle class children, the expectations for success and better preparation of the middle class children help lower class children to raise their own expectations and achievement. This theory seems especially true when the middle class norms predominate.[6] It would follow that if a small group of middle class children were bused to a school where lower class values predominate, the parents of the middle class children may have a realistic basis for concern. If the middle class children accomodate to values of disdain of school achievement, they may lower their expectations and performance.

Although we Americans view ourselves as quite equalitarian, the reality is that our important leaders are increasingly drawn from a literate, well educated and well connected minority. Some political observers fear that we are moving toward a leadership that will become a meritocracy. We must rely increasingly on attorneys, economists, scientists, engineers and a host of other experts to interpret complex laws, defense systems energy alternatives, and tax requirements.

Politically, morality is no simple matter. At the national level we simultaneously believe that we shouldn't interfere in the affairs of other nations except if our interests are threatened, especially national security, or if gross inhumane atrocities are being carried out such as genocide.

Our morality in the economic realm is strongly based on respect for property. Private property is considered a foundation value in capitalism for if a person can't expect to safely hold and enjoy his property--the fruit of his work--then savings and

16

capital wouldn't accumulate. Our surplus above sub-
sistence survival make capitalism and wealth possible.

We also believe that hard work, ingenuity and
prudence should be rewarded. Americans are generous and share by income redistribution through taxes,
welfare and thousands of voluntary organizations including churches, missions, foundations, etc. But
we are impatient and often resent the improvident
"grasshoppers."

The ! Kung Bushmen have been called "The Harmless People" by Elizabeth T. Marshall[7] but recent
study shows that the Bushmen aren't without fights
and even homicides.[8] Nevertheless, they are an attractive, usually congenial people with a well integrated society and have surprisingly equalitarian
relationships with no formal leaders.

Although the environment in which they live
appears harsh and barren,[9] extensive knowledge of
their environment makes it relatively benign and
productive. Their diet consists of meat obtained by
hunting small deer-like steenbok, gemsbok, wild pig,
porcupine and other small animals. In addition to
meat, the staple of their diet is vegetable food.
Most available and accessable is the mongono nut
which is usually gathered by the women, roasted and
then cracked. The nut is rich in protein and other
nutrients. They also gather many other fruits and
nuts such as wild plums. On the average, adults
work about 17 hours per week.

The land is not owned by individuals but considered owned by all. No effort is made to store
food because it is usually plentiful year around.
When a large animal is killed in the hunt, the meat
is shared with relatives, members of the village,
and even neighboring villages.

Social class is non-existent among the Bushmen.
Women are as frequently informal leaders as are men.
The basis for leadership may be age, success in the

hunt for men, physical size and prowess, number of children, etc. But there are no headmen or women.

Religion is an integral part of the social life of a village and about once a month the village will have a feast, a dance and the medicine man will work himself into a trance and bless all members of the village by the laying on of hands along with prayer in the form of a chant. All members of the village receive a blessing, whether young or old, male or female, sick or well.

Religion is naturally interwoven into the fabric of social life and is reasonably coherent and consistent. Children learn the ceremonies and dances by participating, by watching the adults and by gentle guidance from parents. Morality is transmitted mainly by modeling and imitation; exhortation and preaching are rarely observed.

What values make up the morality of the ! Kung?

1. Generosity and sharing.

2. Respect for land and common ownership.

3. Expectation of adequate food through extensive knowledge of their environment.

4. Monogamy and sexual fidelity (usually, but strong sanctions are not brought against violators).

5. Children are esteemed, especially by the women and especially if spaced about three years apart. More closely spaced children are thought to cause a "permanent bachache."

6. Congenial social relations, much talk, humor and laughter.

In the following chart, similarities and differences are juxtaposed for convenience: (SEE CHART #1 ON PAGE 19).

18

CHART #1

Primitive   !Kung Bushmen

Methods of Socialization

Modeling $\longleftrightarrow$ Imitation

Religion - Interwoven, all participate regularly; coherent and consistent

Econ - Work about 17 hours per week on hunting and food gathering; much socializing and leisure. Generous and sharing. Rely on knowledge of environment to harvest environment and regularly find food.

Pol - All participate; seniority may lead to leader positions.

Social Class - Not many differences; for those that exist, it is obvious why:
Stronger
Older
Superior hunter

Some Principle Values -

Having adequate food from day to day
Pleasant social relationships
Sharing and generosity
Children and extended family
Conforming to Bushman way
Cooperation over competition
Equality practiced
Common ownership of land

CHART #1 Continued

Modern   United States

_____

Methods of Socialization

Exhortation	Compliance
Modeling by right adults	Imitation
Formal education	Knowledge

Religion - Removed; pluralistic; diverse; 95% stated belief but less than 50% regular activity; considerable diversity and conflict among Christian religions

Econ - Protestant or Puritan Ethic of hard work, delayed gratification, saving for capital formation; providence

Pol - Representative but increasingly open to those with merit such as literacy, legal training, science, economics and other expertise.

Social Class - Ostensibly classless but in fact is open-class with at least 6 discernable classes.

Some Principle Values -

Living the good life--affluence and working leisure
Human dignity
Freedom
Family without close ties
Conforming to Judeao-Christian and middle class norms
Competition over cooperation
Equality as an ideal
Strict property rights and legal structure

In conclusion, the value systems and morality of ! Kung Bushmen and modern middle class Americans have some surprising similarities and differences. The Bushmen have some attractive values such as their generosity, amicable sociable relationships, and natural way of defusing arguments by humor. In addition, the idea of a seventeen hour work week may sound appealing to many U.S. workers.

As U.S. public schools have increasingly become the prime agencies for social engineering, and also become increasingly violent, the informal and wholestic educational system of the Bushmen may appear attractive.

However, the lack of showers, privacy, and vulnerability to the elements would prevent most Americans from finding anything good about the ! Kung morality and life style.

The major lesson from this chapter is that children can be socialized and can acquire a system of morality that is functional and even admirable without any formal moral education!

CHAPTER III

JEWISH AND EARLY CHRISTIAN MORAL EDUCATION

Our present moral education in the United States comes predominantly from Jewish and Christian ideals. It is easy to underestimate the influence of Judeao-Christian morality in the 1980's because less than half of the population regularly attends church services and this has been interpreted to represent a decline in religion. Then too, because church and school are legally separated in the United States, it is easy to assume that no moral education exists in the public schools.

Certainly modern America is not a Puritan nation. But it should be remembered that about 94% of Americans profess to believe in God according to surveys.[1] Further, Gallup has noted a trend toward "normalcy" with about 90% of all age groups preferring "More Respect for Authority," and "More Emphasis on Traditional Family Ties." About 70% of those surveyed prefer more emphasis on hard work, less emphasis on money, and 74% would like to see less emphasis on marijuana use.[2]

Irregardless of the political party in power or the emphasis on the religious or secular in our society, there are some commonly held values which still constitute a morality for most Americans. Most of us believe in freedom, equality, obedience to legally constituted authority, honesty, charity for the poor, volunteer service to others, and hope for peace. These values and others constitute an informal moral education which most Americans regard as coming from our Judeao-Christian heritage.

The Jewish religion is believed to have started with the creation about 4,000 B.C. The Bible records the account of the creation with man being created in the image of God, with the possibility of becoming like the Gods knowing good from evil. The earth was created so that God's earthly children

23

could gain experience and prove that they would obey
God's commandments. Perhaps the best list of commandments was given by the Hebrew God to Moses, a
prophet, which have become known as the Ten Commandments.

God spoke, and these were his words:
I am the Lord your God who brought you out of
Egypt, out of the land of slavery.

You shall have no other god to set against me.
You shall not make a carved image for yourself
nor the likeness of anything in the heavens
above, or on the earth below, or in the waters
under the earth.

You shall not bow down to worship them; for I,
the Lord your God am a jealous god. I punish
the children for the sins of the fathers to
the third and fourth generations of those who
hate me. But I keep faith with thousands, with
those who love me and keep my commandments.

You shall not make wrong use of the name of the
Lord your God; the Lord will not leave unpun-
ished the man who misuses his name.

Remember to keep the sabbath day holy. You
have six days to labor and do all your work.
But the seventh day is a sabbath day of the
Lord your God; that day you shall not do any
work....

Honour your father and your mother, that you
may live long in the land which the Lord your
God is giving you.

You shall not commit murder.
You shall not commit adultery.
You shall not steal.
You shall not give false evidence against your
neighbour.
You shall not covet your neighbor's house; you

shall not covet your neighbor's wife, his slave, his slave-girl, his ox, his ass, or anything that belongs to him.[3]

The law as given to Moses includes much more detailed instructions about what the people were permitted to do and what was prohibited. Death was the punishment for breaking many of the commandments.

Hebrew moral education came directly from the Talmud which is very detailed and exacting. If humans were to refine themselves enough to achieve a divine dimension, careful attention must be given to the law.[4] Rabbis had the responsibility to know the law and to teach the fundamentals to the young.

The Hebrew God as described by Moses was different from the Gods of other nations of the time. Whereas the Greeks had many Gods who were half God and half human (and therefore capricious), the Hebrew God was a "living God" not a mere mythic god, like the others of the world...."[5] This "living God" talked face to face to Moses and other prophets. Very explicit laws and commandments were given.

With the coming of Christ, the laws of Moses were considered fulfilled by Christians. Morality became obeying the law plus following the spirit and example of Christ. The apostle Matthew describes Christ's words regarding the law:

Think not that I am come to destroy the law, or the prophets: I am not come to destroy, but to fulfill.

For verily I say unto you, Till heaven and earth pass, one jot or one tittle shall in no wise pass from the law, till all be fulfilled.

Whosoever therefore shall break one of these least commandments, and shall teach men so, he shall be called the least in the kingdom of heaven:

but whosoever shall <u>do</u> and teach them,
the same shall be ca<u>ll</u>ed great in the
kingdom of heaven.[6]

The emphasis on the spirit of the law including
becoming meek, merciful, pure in heart and peace
makers in addition to obeying the requirements of the
laws is distinctive in the New Testament. Whereas
the Greeks and Romans found virtue in being good citizens of their nations, early Christians saw themselves as citizens of the Kingdom of God.

Ye have heard that it hath been said,
Thou shalt love thy neighbor, and hate thine
enemy.

But I say unto you, Love your enemies,
bless them that curse you, do good to them
that hate you, and pray for them which
despitefully use you;

That ye may be the children of your
Father which is in heaven: for he maketh
his sun to rise on the evil and on the good,
and sendeth rain on the just and the unjust.[7]

This was a new and difficult doctrine. The
Hebrews expected a savior who would deliver them
from their earthly enemies. Christ left them in
political bondage and then asked them to love their
enemies! It is not surprising that most Hebrews
found no savior in him.

The moral education of early Christianity was
taught by Christ for three years and after his death
was carried on by his disciples. During the first
100 years of Christianity, moral education was probably carried on in small gatherings where little
bands of Christians lived, since neither the Hebrews
nor Romans accepted Christianity nor the Christians.

In the second century after Christ, small catechumenal (schools that taught the <u>catechism</u> and
fundamentals of Christian beliefs) <u>schools began</u>.

26

The first was in Alexandria in 180 A.D. and others followed in Jerusalem, Rome, Antioch, Athens and other cities where Christians lived. These schools were small, informal and often not very organized. Their purpose was to teach adult converts and children to read the Bible. Perhaps the highlight of these schools might have been when some of the early Christian fathers such as Augustine, Eusibius, Origen or Ambrose visited them. These fathers were both theologians and missionaries and often attracted a considerable following of young adults.[8]

If young Christians wanted more education than was available in the catechumenal schools, they had to decide whether to risk going to imperial schools, if they were Romans, with the exposure to pagan doctrines, or to go to monasteries to train to become monks, or to go to catheral schools which developed. As imperial Rome declined in the 5th century A.D. so did the imperial schools. The Christian schools served not only to foster Christian doctrine. but also played an important role in maintaining literacy at least for the few. In later centuries, public schools would arise from the foundations of Christian schools of the early Christian period and the middle ages.

CHAPTER IV

A STUDY OF THE ANCIENTS--
GREEK AND ROMAN MORAL EDUCATION

The foundation for contemporary moral education was provided by the ancient Greeks. Early Greek educational practices were designed to strengthen the state through the proper education of its citizens. The center of the Grecian government was the city-state. Originally, these were no more than patriarchal families united together and living in villages for mutual protection. As these city-states grew, formal education developed for the aristocratic boys, but not for the girls or slaves. It helps to remember that the Greeks were constantly fighting and education was viewed primarily as a means to develop valiant warriors.

Greek education can be conveniently divided into two periods: 1) the old Homeric period (900-500 B.C.) during which education heavily emphasized the molding of the citizen warrior for the good of the state, and 2) the period of transition and decline (500-200 B.C.) during which the emphasis was shifted toward the development of the individual for his own well being while still emphasizing the role of the citizen warrior.

Education during the Homeric period is best portrayed in the epic poems, The Illiad and The Odyssey, written around 900-800 B.C. In these poems, Homer writes about great heroic characters such as Achilles who embodied "an heroic morality of honor"....[1] Greek warriors led short lives and expected to die a quick death in battle. They were consistently striving to be the best, the champion, the victor. However, this wasn't primarily for egocentric purposes but an attempt to achieve the ideal of perfect valor.[2]

Although early Greek education included some instruction in "letters," reading and writing were not a major part of the curriculum. Homer's poems were memorized and recited so that the great ideals within the poems were always before the young men. Each student had a tutor who was responsible for both his education and his character. The tutor was expected to be a model of excellent manhood worthy of emulation by the younger man. Each student worked hard to please his tutor.

The aim of early Greek education was to instill the virtues of valor, courage, responsibility, temperance, self control and allegiance to the state. As time passed, virtue gradually became defined as courage and obedience to the state; this was especially true in Sparta which gradually evolved into a rigid military socialist state. In both Athens and Sparta, physical bravery began to replace wealth and noble birth for advanced standing in citizenship.

The city-states of Athens and Sparta gradually developed into the two most powerful groups in Greece. Military training was required of all young men between 18 to 20 years of age and in Sparta being a good soldier was a life long task. This heavy emphasis on physical prowess and being a dedicated soldier was especially detrimental to family life. The seriousness of the soldier's obligations are illustrated in the following oath taken by prospective Athenian soldiers.

I will never bring reproach upon my hallowed arms nor will I desert the comrade at whose side I stand, but will defend our alters and our hearths, single-handed or supported by many. My native land I will not leave a diminished heritage but greater and better than when I received it. I will obey whoever is in authority and submit to the established laws and all others which the people shall harmoniously enact. If anyone tries to overthrow the constitution or disobeys it, I will not permit him, but

will come to its defense single-handed or with
the support of all. I will honor the religion of my fathers. Let the gods be my wit-
nesses, Agraulus, Enyalius, Ares, Zeus, Thallo,
Auxo, Hegemone.[3]

Although the Euphebic oath was written about 330
B.C. during the second period of Greek education,
valor and state service were still primary virtues.
In paying tribute to Athen's fallen soldiers, Peri-
cles said: "For where the rewards of virtue are
greatest, there the noblest citizens are enlisted
in the service of the state."[4]

However, as time passed, the citizens of Greece
began to think differently. The poor who helped win
the war demanded citizenship rights. Soon, democracy
flourished and freedom of expression was at its
height. Increased wealth brought increased leisure
time. Intellectual power replaced military ability
as a prerequisite to leadership. New ideas were tol-
erated. Perhaps the greatest change in Grecian culture and society was the new emphasis on individualism
rather than the old subordination of the individual
to the state.

In early Greek culture ideals such as Right and
Justice and Truth were seen as eternal laws of the
universe. Hesiod (c. 700 B.C.) thought of justice as
an ideal which was an object of faith grounded in the
very nature of the universe, and not subject to the
whims of the Olympian gods. He thought that right-
eousness and work were the foundations of arete which
means excellence.[5] The concept of the ideal man and
universal laws shaped the thinking of the philosophers, educators, poets, artists and soldiers.

But about the 5th Century B.C. a new group of
teachers arose called the Sophists. The Sophists made
important contributions to Athenian education through
emphasis on public speaking.

They became the first lawyers of modern
civilization. To the Sophists, the humanities

31

were the core of education. But as skeptics, they opposed absolutism. Thus, Gorgias taught:
1. Nothing (Absolute) exists.
2. Even if it existed, it could not be known.
3. Even if it could be known, it could not be communicated.[6]

The Sophists put great emphasis on individuality because each person could interpret things himself since there were no absolutes. Because they were critical and probably disruptive of unity, they aroused opposition.

Socrates (470-399 B.C.) disagreed with the Sophists and found value in the older teachings. Like Hesiod, he sought for the underlying idea or spiritual principle. He thought that knowledge possessed a universal validity and could be arrived at by thoughtful conversation and discourse. Because knowledge was truth, it was only another step for Socrates to assert that "Knowledge is virtue."[7]

Socrates was convinced that some aspects of the older Greek education such as the patriotism and service to the state should be preserved. He had been a brave soldier on many occasions, and became concerned with the excessive individualism advocated by the Sophists. His method of teaching was to engage in the most probing kind of discussions with the young aristocrats of Athens. He thought that such discussions would help to develop their power of thought, would help to discover or clarify truth, and would help them to become more moral, responsible and pious. When asked to stop teaching the youth or leave Athens, Socrates said:

> Perhaps someone will say, "Why cannot you withdraw from Athens, Socrates, and hold your peace?" It is the most difficult thing in the world to make you understand why I cannot do that. If I say that I cannot hold my peace because that would be to disobey the god, you will think that I am not in earnest and will not believe me. And if I tell you that no greater good can happen to a man than to discuss human excellence every day and the other matters

32

about which you have heard me arguing and examining myself and others, and that an unexamined
life is not worth living, then you will believe
me still less."[8]

However, the officials of Athens found Socrates too
much a gadfly and he was tried for corrupting the
youth, sentenced, and died by drinking poison hemlock.

Plato (c. 427-346 B.C.) was Socrates' student and
chronicler. Like Socrates, Plato believed in the traditional Greek values, and was even critical of the
bad example set by the gods in the Homeric poems.
To Plato, the Homeric poems showed the gods having
human weakness and he objected to the bad examples
the gods set:

> . . . the young man should not be told that in
> committing the worst of crimes he is far from
> doing anything outrageous; and that if he
> chastises his father when he does wrong, in
> any manner that he likes, he will only be fol-
> lowing the example of the first and greatest
> among the gods.[9]

Many of the tales in Homer's poems portrayed the gods
doing evil toward their fathers or mothers. Even
though these taught lessons of courage or bravery,
Plato felt that their influence upon children would
be unfavorable. In this same conversation Socrates
said:

> For the young man cannot judge what is alle-
> gorical and what is literal; anything that
> he receives into his mind at that age is apt
> to become indelible and unalterable: and
> therefore the tales which they first hear
> should be models of virtuous thoughts.[10]

Teachers of youth, he felt, must guide children into
imitating good behavior and in so doing it will become a part of their personalities.[11]

In all these examples concerning the education of
youth in moral behavior, we see that education is still
very regimented. In the Republic, society is governed

by a ruling class of philosophers. These men, Plato felt, could best govern society because of their wisdom. These guardians would see that only virtuous conduct was taught. Rules and legal codes were set up to insure that proper behavior existed. However, Plato believed that as individuals became more educated in proper moral conduct, they would begin to govern themselves and require less regimentation.[12]

Plato's influence upon educational thought was immense. Moral education taught in the schools meant that society would be moral. This faith in the power of moral education continued to be expanded from ancient times throughout the Middle Ages and the Renaissance Period even into our day.

Another Greek philosopher who expanded this theory for later generations and centuries was Aristotle. Like Plato, Aristotle viewed education for the development of society as well as the individual. He saw the power of education in youth. In his Politics, he talks about the relationship between education and the state.

No one will doubt that the legislator should direct his attention above all to the education of youth, or that the neglect of education does harm to states. The citizen should be moulded to suit the form of government under which he lives. For each government has a peculiar character which originally formed and which continues to preserve it. The character of democracy creates democracy and the character of oligarchy creates oligarchy; and always the better the character, the better the government.[13]

Aristotle's foundation of education started in the home. Children should be protected from bad influences of the outside world as well as the bad examples which might be observed in the home.

For until they are seven years old they must live at home; and therefore, even at this early age, all that is mean and low should be banished from their sight and hearing. Indeed, there is

34

nothing which the legislator should be more
careful to drive away than indecency of
speech; for the light utterance of shameful
words is akin to shameful actions. The young
especially should never be allowed to repeat
or hear anything of the sort. . . . But the
legislator should not allow youth to be
hearers of satirical Iambic verses or spec-
tators of comedy until they are of an age
to sit at the public tables and to drink strong
wine; by that time education will have armed
them against the evil influences of such repre-
sentations. . . . And therefore youth should
be kept strangers to all that is bad, and
especially to things which suggest vice or
hate.[14]

After the age of seven, children start their formal
education. Aristotle entertained the question of
whether or not education should be "more concerned
with intellectual or moral virtue."[15]

To Aristotle, both were necessary. But Aristotle
believed that character must be more than mere instruction. "Some think we are made good by nature,
others by habitation, others by teaching."[16] He held
that knowledge is of little value in making men good.
He said: "If it be a question of possessing the virtues, the mere knowledge is of little or no avail."[17]
Notice this change from the view of Socrates. Knowledge of good does not necessarily mean that one wishes
it. Aristotle felt that virtue must be desired. "It
is not enough to know the nature of virtue," he explains, "we must endeavor to possess it, and use whatever other means are necessary for becoming good."[18]
Moral education to Aristotle was more the development
of habits rather than the teaching of theories. This
theory of moral education continued later in history
as men have pondered about the correct methods in
helping others to acquire moral habits.

As Greek culture spread throughout the Mediter-
ranean, new educational institutions grew up. The
Sophists' influence helped develop philosophical and

rhetorical schools with oratory training developed in the rhetorical schools. Plato and Aristotle had organized their students into schools and eventually universities grew out of these schools. With the conquest of Greeks by the Romans in 146 B.C., these schools and universities were made part of the Roman education. [19]

Names such as Tacitus, Quintilian and Cicero emerge as we review some of the great theoretical discussions of education in Rome. To understand the type of moral education taught in Rome, we can turn to the oratories and writings of two men.

Cicero (106-43 B.C.) was a great orator, philosopher, and statesman in Rome who published many works on political, philosophical, and historical subjects. In addition to these, he also published treatises on rhetoric. While all of these works reflected Cicero's theory of education, his most important educational work was De Oratore. The orator, to the Roman, was the educated man who participated in the affairs of the state. The Roman orator, Monroe says, included "the teacher, the publicist, the religious teacher . . . devoted to legal, judicial, or legislative activities . . . ."[20] De Oratore is written in dialogue form (like many early Greek and Roman literary works) and gives Cicero's views on oratory and education. Perhaps an even greater discussion on education and oratory is given in Quintilian's De Institutione Oratoria.

Marcus Fabius Quintilainus was born about 35 A.D. in Spain but was educated in Rome. In De Institutione Oratoria, he expresses his thought about moral education. Here he condemns the morals of society and blames negligent parents and teachers. We also can see a glimpse of what the Roman Empire might have been like as it started to decline:

We enervate their very infancy with luxuries. That delicacy of education, which we call fondness, weakens all the powers, both of body and mind. What luxury will he not

36

covet in his manhood, who crawls about on
purple! He cannot yet articulate his first
words, when he already distinguishes scarlet,
and wants his purple. We form the palate of
children before we form their pronunciation.
They grow up in sedan chairs; if they touch
the ground, they hang by the hands of atten-
dants supporting them on each side. We are
delighted if they utter anything immodest. . . .
From such practices springs habit, and after-
wards nature. The unfortunate children learn
these vices before they know that they are
vices. . . .[21]

Quintilian was very concerned about the morals of
Roman society and goes on to describe what kind of
moral education should be taught. He suggests that
parents be very careful in choosing a teacher and
explains that teachers, whether tutors or professors,
should be men of morality and integrity. Quintilian
thought that it was especially important that the
teachers of younger boys not only set a good example,
but also that teachers should require their students
to be moral, using strict and severe discipline if
necessary. The ideal teacher would be like a concerned
parent who expected the best of his sons, who lays
ideals before them, and insists that they be better
than the norm of the aristocratic society in which
they lived. [22]

In both Greek and Roman societies, during the
early formative periods (about 800-550 B.C. for the
Greeks, and about 250-100 B.C. for the Romans) parents played an important role in the immediate life
and education of their children. But as these societies became strong, wealthy, and leisure time became available for at least the aristocrats, education was transferred from the parents to tutors and
teachers. Plutarch describes Cato as a commendable
father. Cato lived from 234-149 B.C. in the early
period.

As soon as he had a son born. . . he
would be by when his wife washed it, and
dressed it. . . . When he began to come to
years of discretion, Cato himself would teach

37

him to read, although he had a servant,
a very good grammarian, called Chilo,
who taught many others.

    Cato taught his son history, geogra-
phy, swimming, boxing, law, grammar and
gymnastics. He was especially careful
to never speak anything obscene in his son's
presence.

    "Thus, like an excellent work, Cato
formed and fashioned his son to virtue. . . .[23]

Moral education in a decadent society is always
difficult and was especially so in Rome during the
period of the empire.

    The classroom behaviour of boys and youths,
when rhetorical exercises were being decalimed,
too often illustrated the effects of an indul-
gent, or careless and undisciplined, home up-
bringing. . . .The boys, . . . learnt to
despise hard work, became brazenly self-assured,
and made their faults worse by constantly repeating them. Such were the conditions which
teachers like Quintilian sought to combat as
best they could; but the underlying cause lay
in the fact that many of these boys came from
homes where they had either been spoiled, or
ill-controlled, or encouraged by over-ambitious
parents to premature exhibition of their abilities.[24]

Although we have inherited much of value from
Rome culture, Roman moral education in the later
periods shows us much to avoid rather than emulate.

Preachers, scholars and even economists have
speculated about the fall of Rome after the second
century A.D. Mayer makes a good case that a poor
educational system helped the decline as much as anything. Whereas the Greeks emphasized public service
as self discipline, the Romans had little ideal of
public service and self discipline. In addition, the

Romans didn't have the philosophical thinkers such as Plato and Aristotle to provide the base for education.[24]

Rostovtzeff maintains that the Roman decline was due to economic inflation. Rome was a parasitic city whose chief product was government. Some emperors fueled inflation by debasing the currency--by creating money wrecklessly. Diocletian and Constantine imposed artificial economic controls in an effort to fight inflation. Continuing inflation led to a loss of morale among the population and also led to an economic caste system; there were a small minority of wealthy families who profited from the economic difficulties but most became increasingly impoverished.[25]

Another contribution to Rome's decline may have been the loss of focus or lack of clear national objectives and purposes. Emile Durkheim, the great French sociologist was convinced that:

. . . Society must, in addition, have before it an ideal toward which it reaches. It must have some good to achieve, an original contribution to bring to the moral patrimony of mankind. Idleness is a bad counselor for collectivities as well as individuals. When individual activity does not know where to take hold, it turns against itself. When the moral forces of a society remain unemployed, when they are not engaged in some work to accomplish, they deviate from their moral sense and are used up in a morbid and harmful manner.[26]

First Rome adopted the Greek philosophies, then the mystery cults, then embraced Christianity. During the period of the empire, Rome was overextended both politically and economically. But a clear sense of purpose eluded the Romans and that was reflected in their moral education.

In summary, moral education in both Greek and Roman societies was simple, family centered and admirable in early periods. As each society became successful in war and commerce, education for the children of the aristocrats was moved from the family to tutors and schools. Great thinkers and educators fought to preserve the best of their culture and maintain high standards for their pupils. But engulfing events outside the schools brought great changes and new eras.

CHAPTER V

CHRISTIAN EDUCATION IN THE
EARLY MIDDLE AGES

The teachings of Christ and his followers produced an entirely different concept in moral education. Virtue did not center around man's relationship with the state but rather his relationship to a Supreme Being. Instead of seeking personal happiness (as seen in later Greek and Roman culture) men sought happiness in serving one another. These teachings produced the foundation of moral education. In the two or three centuries following Christ, the Church began to formalize its teachings. Catechetical schools were established to instruct those anticipating membership in the Church. These schools became the educational institutions of the early middle ages and concentrated on the moral training of its members. Other church schools emerged which specifically trained the clergy. Some of the instruction in these schools were taken from the works of Clement and Origen. Clement, who had studied Plato extensively, became a Christian and interpreted Christian teachings from the perspective of Platonic philosophy. Origen, a student of Clement, contributed to the development of these "theological" schools by intellectualizing and examining Christian teachings. An example of Origen's writings gives a glimpse of what kind of moral instruction was taught. In this example, Origen is examining the question of what happens to those who do not follow a proper life:

> Those on the other hand, who do not yet offer themselves to God with such constancy and affection, and are not ready to come into His service, and to prepare their souls for trial, are said to be abandoned by God, i.e. not to be instructed, inasmuch as they are not prepared for instruction, their training or care being undoubtedly postponed to a later time. These certainly do not know what they will obtain from God, unless they first

entertain the desire of being benefited;
and this finally will be the case, if a
man come first to a knowledge of himself,
and feel what are his defects, and understand from whom he either ought or can
seek the supply of his deficiencies. For
he who does not know beforehand of his
weakness or his sickness, cannot seek a
physician; or at least, after recovering
his health, that man will not be grateful
to his physician who did not first recog-
nise the dangerous nature of his ailment.
And so, unless a man has first ascertained
the defects of his life, and the evil nature
of his sins, and made this known by con-
fession from his own lips, he cannot be
cleansed or acquitted, lest he should be
ignorant that what he possesses has been
bestowed on him by favour, but should
consider as his own property what flows
from the divine liberality, which idea
undoubtedly generates arrogance of mind
and pride, and finally, becomes the cause
of the individual's ruin.[1]

Perhaps those schools with which most are ac-
quainted during the early middle ages were the mon-
astaries. Monastic education was characterized by
emphasis upon denial. Rigid rules were formulated
which stressed ideals of chastity, poverty, and obedience. In E. P. Cubberley's book, Readings in the
History of Education, which is a collection of original sources in the development of education, an
example is given of the Monastic Vow. Here we find
some of those monastic ideals expressed:

I hereby renounce my parents, my
brothers and relatives, my friends, my
possessions and my property, and the vain
and empty glory and pleasure of this world.
I also renounce my own will, for the will
of God. I accept all the hardships of the
monastic life, and take the vows of purity,

42

chastity, and poverty, in the hope of heaven;
and I promise to remain a monk in this mona-
stery all the days of my life.[2]

The moral values expressed in monastacism influenced
society as a whole. Monasteries became the only
schools for teaching in the early middle ages. They
preserved the writings of the ancients and had the
only libraries. At first, most of their teachings
were in religious instruction; however, by the sixth
and seventh centuries their curriculum expanded.

The monastic schools began to develop into two
separate schools with two separate purposes. One
school system was developed for those who were entering
the priesthood, the other for lay members of the Church.
The instruction in both was slight but it did provide
instruction in reading and writing. Of course, most
of the instruction was still heavy on religious observance and conduct, but gradually emphasis shifted
to a more general education. In 787 A.D., Charle-
magne recognized the need for a broader education and
directed the abbots of the monasteries in the frankish
kingdom to teach capable students the scriptures, lessons in morality, how to speak correctly, and how to
read and write.[3]

As learning increased, the curriculum was en-
larged to include other disciplines. After students
learned the basic skills, they advanced to a broader
range of studies. These advanced studies became
known as the seven Liberal Arts. These were separated
into two divisions: 1) The Trivium and; 2) The
Quadrivium. The first division included grammar,
rhetoric, and dialetic; while the second division incorporated studies in arithmetic, geometry, astronomy,
and music.[4]

The Seven Liberal Arts represented an expansion
in learning but theology and moral conduct were still
the main focal points. This is evident as we read
Rabanus Maurus' (776-856 A.D.) explanation of the
Seven Liberal Arts in his Education of the Clergy.

43

Maurus was an educated clergyman and an abbot. The following includes some selections from an extract written in 819.

The Holy Scripture

The foundation, the content, and the perfection of all wisdom is Holy Scripture. . . .

The Liberal Arts

The first of the liberal arts is grammar, the second rhetoric, the third dialectic, the fourth arithmetic, the fifth geometry, the sixth music, and the seventh astronomy. . . . Grammar is the source and foundation of the liberal arts. . . . Rhetoric is the art of using secular discourse affectively in the circumstances of daily life.[5]

Teaching from the scriptures implies that moral ideas were taught. However, when the scriptures were not used, teachers were very careful to use literature which taught principles. Paul Abelson in his study of the Seven Liberal Arts points out that books besides the scriptures usually were a compilation of fables and folklore. He states:

Although every teacher was practically compelled to compile his own reading book, they all used similar material. They seemed to have had a common appreciation of a pedagogical situation which they all met in approximately the same fashion. . . . .modern historians have brought to light a vast number of these productions. Some, though representing the labor of a teacher's lifetime, probably never obtained popularity outside of the school in which the author taught; others enjoyed a wider celebrity and were often in use in widely scattered places; a few were known throughout Christendom. . . .Fables, folklore, biblical proverbs, characteristic national proverbs, facts of every day interest,

particularly to a schoolboy--all these make
up the content of the host of these little
medieval readers. [6]

The prime purpose of these medieval "primers" was
to teach reading with proper moral content. Some of
the best examples of these fables and folklore are
found in the Tales of the Monks from the Gesta Romanorum. The Gesta Romanorum was a compilation of
stories and fables originally intended to serve as a
manual for the clergy. Compiled to illustrate moral
and religious virtue, they were most likely used by
the clergy in teaching their students. [7] Notice the
moral lessons taught in the following tale.

"Engraved Upon An Ancient Tomb":

We read of a certain Roman Emperor, who built
a magnificent palace. In digging the foundation, the workmen discovered a golden coffin,
ornamented with three circlets, on which were
inscribed, "I have expended--I have given--I
have kept--I have possessed--I do possess--
I have lost--I am punished. What I formerly
expended, I have; what I gave away, I have."
    The emperor, on seeing this, called to
him the nobles of his empire, and said, "Go,
and consider among ye what this inscription
signifies."
    The noblemen replied, "Sire, the meaning
is, that an emperor, who reigned before your
majesty, wished to leave an example for the
imitation of his successors. He therefore
wrote, 'I have expended, '--that is, my life;
judging some, admonishing others, and governing
to the best of my ability. 'I have given,
'--that is, equipments to my soldiers, and
supplies to the needy; to every one according
to his desert. 'I have kept, '--that is,
exact justice; showing mercy to the indigent,
and yielding to the labourer his hire. 'I
have possessed, '--that is, a generous and

45

true heart; recompensing faithfully those
who have done me service, and exhibiting
at all time a kind and affable exterior.
'I do possess, '--that is, a hand to bestow,
to protect, and to punish. 'I have lost,
'--that is, my folly; I have lost the
friendship of my foes, and the lascivious
indulgences of the flesh. 'I am punished,
'--that is in hell; because I believed
not in one eternal God, and put no faith
in the redemption."

The emperor hearing this, ever after reg-
ulated himself and his subjects with greater
wisdom, and finished his life in peace.[8]

This tale is an excellent illustration of moral and
religious values placed upon society (especially the
clergy) in the educational process.

Maurus points out that knowledge in other areas
is essential for the good health of the Church. This
selection is taken from his treatise, The Education
of the Clergy.

An ecclesiastical education should
qualify the sacred office of the ministry
for divine service. It is fitting that
those who from an exalted station undertake
the direction of the life of the church
should acquire fullness of knowledge, and
that they further should strive after recti-
tude of life and perfection of development.
They should not be allowed to remain in
ignorance of anything that appears beneficial for their own information or for the
instruction of those entrusted to their
care. Therefore they should endeavor to
grasp and include in their knowledge the
following things: an acquaintance with
Holy Scripture, the unadulterated truth
of history, the derivative modes of speech,
the mystical sense of words, the advantages
growing out of the separate branches of
knowledge, the integrity of life that

46

manifests itself in good morals, delicacy
and good taste in oral discourse, penetra-
tion in the explanation of doctrine, the
different kinds of medicine, and the
various forms of disease. Anyone to whom
all this remains unknown is not able to
care for his own welfare, let alone that
of others. . . .[9]

The main reason for this increased emphasis on
secular learning was still to strengthen the Church.
The shift toward the development of intellectual
power was by no means a shift away from moral and
religious teaching. Scholasticism, as it came to be
known, attempted to organize other knowledge and make
it consistent with moral and spiritual teaching.

The scholars of this movement sought to develop
intellectual reason in order to understand religious
faith. They used logic as a means of explaining moral
and religious doctrine. Edward J. Power explains the
aim of the scholastics which helps us understand their
purposes:

They began with a determination to
maintain intact the teachings of the Church,
and employed all the formulas of logic to
make reason, as well as the corpus of
classical knowledge, reinforce the doctrines
of their faith. In some fields of knowledge
this purpose was achieved more easily than
in others, for logic could be a servant to
theology by explaining rational connections
between the several parts of dogma, and it
could produce, by clever dialectic, artful
distinction, and prudent synthesis, a
philosophy consistent with theological doctrine.[10]

The increased interest in logic and reason at some
monasteries helped to develop them into great centers
of learning. These became the great universities of
that time period, and as they grew, they became less
attached to the strict monastic orders. The educational system fell into the hands of some of the

freer orders in the Church. Two of the better known were the Franciscan and Dominican orders.

The universities' role became more secular even as the Church continued to control its activities. P. R. Cole writes in his History of Educational Thought:

> The medieval universities remained under ecclesiastical control; but were less exclusively clerical than the old monastic and cathedral schools. Cities and monarchs shared in their foundation; and their government tended towards autonomy. Meanwhile the Church still held the monopoly of the licence to teach, and regulated the dress and mode of life of masters and pupils alike. The masters still held ecclesiastical offices, while the students enjoyed clerical privileges, and in most cases contemplated a clerical career. . . . .The elements of the university curriculum in the Middle Ages may be defined as theology, Aristotle, civil and cannon law, the seven liberal arts, and medicine. The focus of greatest interest was certainly the scholastic theology.[11]

In addition to theological teachings in the university curriculum, another institution outside of the university played an important role in the moral education of society. This institution was chivalry. Chivalry performed the function of schooling the nobility in Christian manners and bravery primarily in defense of the Church. A knight was a "Christian soldier" whose duty was to defend the Church and protect the down trodden. He was to maintain strict standards in his personal life but was to be in the world, unlike most monks.[12]

The influence of chivalry in education was indirect. Those literary men of the later middle ages who wrote about the art of Chivalry helped to propagate its ideals. But education was still for the select and the ideals of chivalry did not reach the common people.

The literary books used in the universities were very narrow in scope. Even though the new orders were freer than the old monastic masters, they still were careful to regulate the types of literature which could be studied. In 1228 A.D., the Dominican Order published a statement concerning studies in the schools under their jurisdiction. The following describes the types of literature which could be used.

> They shall not study in the books of the Gentiles and philosophers, although they may inspect them briefly. They shall not learn secular sciences nor even the arts which are called liberal, unless sometimes in certain cases the master of the Order or the general chapter shall wish to make a dispensation, but shall read only theological works whether they be youths or others. Moreover, we have decreed that each province shall provide for its brothers sent to the university at least three books of theology, and the brothers sent to the university shall study histories and sentences, and text and glosses especially.[13]

Many books were strictly forbidden. Aristotle's writings on natural philosophy were not to read "in public or secret" as decreed by the Bishops of the Church.[14]

Again, it must be remembered that education was not universal in the middle ages. If a general education could not be obtained, the Church made sure that at least a rudimentary religious education was given. In England in the 13th and 14th centuries, parish priests were instructed to take care that boys knew the Lord's Prayer, the Creed, the Salutation of the Virgin and how to make the sign of the cross.[15]

Eventually, the moral and religious education of those who attended schools and universities began to change. Perhaps the biggest change was that it became more abstract and philosophical. Roger Bacon, an English monk, wrote in his Opera Inedita (1292) how the religious education of the theologian began to be an exercise in philosophy rather than theology. Even though such works were of a philosophical rather than a practical nature, they still provided moral instruction to the theologian. But even then, there was a scarcity of books of morals.[16]

Eventually moral and religious training became a training in philosophical reasoning. Theological questions were answered from the philosophical writings of the ancient Greeks and Romans.

It is our observation that the Early Christian spiritual and theological training, while maintaining sin, God's law, etc., was concerned more with the spirit than with the moral conduct. In terms of effective moral education for conduct, this period was probably at a historical low, except perhaps the training in chivalry. Moral education became more scientific. This renewed interest in the study of the ancients was a revival of learning and became the Renaissance.

CHAPTER VI

THE RENAISSANCE--A RENEWED INTEREST
IN CLASSICAL THOUGHT

The revival of learning in Europe meant a renewed interest in the classics. The educators of
this period drew heavily upon the educational
theories of the Ancients. Now men, like the ancient Greeks and Romans, focused many of their
thoughts on the moral educaton of society. The
resounding thought of many educators was the inti-
mate relationship between knowledge and moral behavior. This feeling is best expressed by Jacob
Wimpheling, a humanist educator from Germany, in
the following selection from his work Adolescentia.

> Of what use are all of the books of
> the world, the most learned writings, the
> profoundest researchers, if they only
> minister to the vainglory of their authors,
> and do not or cannot advance the good of
> mankind? . . . What profits all our
> learning, if our character be not cor-
> respondingly noble, or our industry with-
> out piety, or our knowing without love
> of our neighbour, or our wisdom without
> humility, or our studying if we were not
> kind and charitable?[1]

Many felt that an increased awareness of the world
as experienced through education would (or should)
have a taming or at least a beneficial influence
upon youth. Major emphasis was placed on developing the scholar who was educated in secular
learning as well as manners and the Christian life.

Desiderus Erasmus, perhaps the most famous educational theorist of the Renaissance, wrote in The
Education of a Christian Prince about the proper
moral education and example of the Christian prince.
The influence of this book was felt primarily by
the noble class. However, other parts of society

51

were no doubt influenced. In his work, Erasmus
quoted from Plutarch's A Philosopher is to Converse with Great Men: "A country owes everything
to a good prince; him it owes to the man who made
him such by his moral principles."[2] The moral
principles taught by the educator (whether parent
or teacher) must begin early. He elaborates:

> There is no better time to shape and
> improve a prince than when he does not yet
> realize himself a prince. This time must
> be diligently employed, not only to the
> end that for a while he may be kept away
> from base associations, but also that he
> may be imbued with certain definite moral
> principles. If diligent parents raise
> with great care a boy who is destined to
> inherit only an acre or two, think how much
> interest and concern should be given to the
> education of one who will succeed not to a
> single dwelling, but to so many peoples, to
> so many cities, yea, to the world, either
> as a good man for the common gain of all,
> or an evil one, to the great ruination of
> all![3]

Erasmus felt that the impetus for the education
of the child must first come from the parents and
was concerned that this responsibility was not being
met. Because of this, the development of moral
conduct was also being neglected. Under the subject
heading, "Parents Will Not See That in Their Children's Interest, Education Matters Most" in De
Pueris Instituendis, Erasmus made these comments
about the parents' negligence in these matters:

> Yet we see a father, who bestows no
> little heed to ensure that his horse and
> dogs are of the right breed, careless
> whether his son be properly trained that
> he may prove an honour to his parents,
> and helpful to them in their later years,
> a worthy husband, a brave and useful
> citizen. Yet for whom does such a father

52

plant and build? For whose behoof does
he contrive wealth by land and by sea?
For his children, forsooth. But what
profit or honour lies in inheriting
such things if their possessor has no
skill to use them aright? Who will
fashion ingeniously a harp for one who
has not learnt to play upon it? Or
furnish a library for one who knows
or cares nothing for books? Why, therefore, heap up riches for one who knows
not how to employ them? For note this
well: that he who provides for a son
who is worthily educated, provides
means to virtue: but whoso saves for
a child, endowed with rude temper and
uncultivated wit is but ministering to
opportunities of indulgence and mis-
chief. It is the height of folly that
one should train the body to be comely,
and wholly neglect that excellence of
mind which alone can guide it aright.
For I hesitate not to affirm that those
things which men covet for their sons--
health, riches, and repute--are more
surely secured by virtue and learning--
the gifts of education--than by any other
means. True, the highest gifts of all
no man can give to another, even to his
child; but we can store his mind with
that sound wisdom and learning whereby
he may attain to the best.[4]

To help supply the proper education for their
children, Erasmus counsels parents to employ
teachers who instruct their children in proper
moral character. In The Education of a Christian
Prince Erasmus defines part of the duties of the
teacher. Note the emphasis again on meeting this
need while the child is young.

The teacher should enter at once upon
his duties, so as to implant the seeds of
good moral conduct while the sense of the
prince are still in the tenderness of

53

youth, while his mind is furthest removed
from all vices and tractably yields to the
hand of guidance in whatever it directs.[5]

In this same quotation Erasmus suggests that teachers
use ". . . pretty stories, pleasing fables, (and)
clever parables," in teaching younger children.

Throughout the Renaissance, like other time
periods, educators continually stressed the importance of using fables and stories in teaching
youth a proper moral example. Underscoring the
Christian education of the Prince, Erasmus taught
that ". . . before all else the story of Christ
must be firmly rooted in the mind of the prince."
The teachings of Christ and the stories from scripture were paramount in forming a moral education
for youth.

Throughout the writings of Erasmus, as well as
others, the elements of a moral life were constantly
stressed. Virtue, moral responsibility, avoidance
of base desires and proper example for others,
helped to form an outline of proper conduct. Everything must be measured by the "Christian standard."
Others expressed similar thoughts. Clara P. McMahon
wrote a book on Education in England in the fifteenth
century. Included in her work is a selection on the
education of girls of noble birth written by a Knight
to his daughters. Here again, the Christian standards of moral conduct are given. In the introduction the Knight of La Tour Landry writes:

I purposed to make a little book in
which I could write the good conditions
and deeds of ladies and gentlewoman . . .
to the intent that my daughters should
take example of fair continuance and good
manners . . . whereupon they might learn
and see both good and evil of the time
past, and for to keep them in good clean-
ness, and from all evil in the time
coming . . . .[6]

54

McMahon points out that included in this work are
"meaty stories, morals, and words of wisdom, with
examples drawn from the Bible, stories of saints . . .
as well as famous classical stories." All the
traits of moral conduct are explained along with
warnings to avoid vices of immorality, etc.

The ideals of education during the Renaissance included other elements besides a moral education. The revival of learning was also a revolt
against the old monastic educational practices.
These ideals of education were sometimes hostilely
opposed to the Church. Cordasco points out that
Renaissance humanism combined with the Reformation
movement, caused most schools to be always concerned with some form of religious reformation and
moral teaching. Thus we turn to the next chapter.

CHAPTER VII

REFORMATION--THE MORAL AND RELIGIOUS
EDUCATIONAL THEORIES OF LUTHER

Martin Luther's publication (1517) of the "95 Theses" started the age of religious reform. However, many events preceding Luther's publication helped bring about the schism in the Catholic Church and the Reformation. For example, John Wycliff, an Oxford scholar and popular clergyman, a century and a half before the German Martin Luther, revolted against the authority of the Pope and the Catholic Church. Wycliff objected to the changes in the Church. He even went so far as to call the Pope and other leaders in the Church as enemies of Christ.

Wycliff's followers and many others throughout Europe saw the Pope becoming more of an earthly prince rather than a spiritual leader. The practice of dispensing indulgences to sinners by priests and the Pope was perhaps most objectionable to young Luther.

Luther's main contention was that the Holy Scriptures should be used to dispel some of these false ideas which permeated the Church. It was the common man who became the center of attention in the Reformation. H. G. Wells, the great historian, wrote in his comprehensive history:

> The general drift of the common man
> in this period in Europe was to set up
> his new acquisition, the Bible, as the
> counter authority to the Church.[1]

Education of the common man was paramount in helping him use his new acquisition. Because the scriptures were the primary instrument in education, moral and religious teachings were the natural outgrowth. The ideal Christian was the individual who taught and lived moral conduct. Moral education was taught through the examples in scripture and expressed in religious creeds. The Bible provided the source of all truth and was used to combat unfounded habits and customs of the Catholic Church. Where untruths were exposed and scriptural truth given, the moral and Christian individual developed.

Most of the moral and religious educational theories developed by the reformers (particularly Luther) were restatements of moral educators of the past, but with heavy emphasis on religious doctrine and scriptural references. The best examples of the moral and religious educational ideas of the Reformation were proposed by the Reformers themselves; the best examples are found in the writings of Luther.

Throughout history up to the advent of Luther, the Catholic Church controlled virtually all education. Now with this authority challenged and usurped in many areas in Europe, the control of education fell upon others. Frederick Eby in his book Early Protestant Educators on the educational writings of Luther and John Calvin points out:

. . . Lutheranism swept away all the ecclesiastical officials, leaving Germany without any authorities to establish, support, and control churches and schools. To meet this threatening situation Luther turned to the secular authorities that had undertaken for several centuries to promote popular schools, the mayors and councilmen of Germany.[2]

Luther saw the importance of persuading civil authorities and parents about the need and benefits of education for the youth. Most of his reasons were founded on moral and religious ideals. When instructing parents on their duties as parents, he said:

. . . For instance, they need both that you teach them that which they do not know of God, and also that you punish them when they

58

will not retain this knowledge. Where-
fore, see to it, that you cause your
children first to be instructed in
spiritual things,--that you point them
first to God, and after that, to the
world. But in these days, this order,
sad to say, is inverted.[3]

Luther admonished parents to train their children correctly in the Lord, encouraging them to
exercise correct conduct so that they (the parents)
might be a good example to their children.

There are others who destroy their
children by using foul language and oaths
in their presence, or by a corrupt demeanor
and example. . . . There are some who are
exceedingly well pleased if their sons
betray a fierce and warlike spirit, and
are ever ready to give blows, as though
it were a great merit in them to show no
fear of any one. . . Again, children are
sufficiently inclined to give way to
anger and evil passions, and hence it
behooves parents to remove temptation
from them, as far as possible, by a
well-guarded example in themselves, both
in words and in actions. For what can
the child of a man, whose language is
habitually vile and profane, be expected
to learn, unless it be the like vileness
and profanity?[4]

A moral and religious education, Luther felt,
not only would help the children but also help the
whole society. In Luther's work, "Family Government the Foundation of All Government" (1525),
he views the proper society as one founded on the
correct governing of the family within the single
household. Luther was convinced that if parents,
especially the father, were kind but strict rulers
in their households, homes would be orderly. If
homes were law abiding and children were obedient,
then neighborhoods, towns and whole nations would

be virtuous, well governed, and prosperous.[5]

In his educational theories we find that
Luther condemned many of the thoughts and ideas
propounded in Aristotle's works. These ideas
Luther felt went contrary to the teachings found
in the Bible. He found the universities badly
in need of reform. The writings of Aristotle had
come to predominate over the teachings of Christ
to such a degree that Luther advocating abandoning
Aristotle altogether. For him, the universities
were places of "dissolute living," "Greek fashion,"
and "heathen manners." Luther blamed the Pope,
the bishops and the prelates for permitting the
universities to be secularized, and for ignoring
the scriptures and scriptural morality.[6]

Luther's contributions to education are immense.
Since the benefits of education were both temperal
and spiritual in Luther's eyes, he sought to acquaint
all children with education. In addition to the
stability it brought society, it also brought eternal
happiness to the individual. Because the scriptures
were essential to eternal salvation in the reformers'
eyes, education was essential so that the individual
might read and comprehend this important text. The
scriptures and education were intertwined and the
outcome was a moral and religious education for the
Christian citizen.

Other prostestant reformers made important contributions to moral education by insisting that the
Bible could be read and followed by everyone. That
not only brought moral codes closer to the common
people but also added an important reason for everyone to learn to read.

CHAPTER VIII

REALISM: A SCIENTIFIC AND PHILOSOPHICAL
APPROACH TO EDUCATION

Up to this time, a strong emphasis had been
placed on the use of literature in the content of
moral education. Usually, the intellectual literature centered around the study of great authors.
During the Renaissance, educators were interested
in the study of the writings of the Ancient Greeks
and Romans, while during the Reformation, educators
centered their moral education around scripture.
However, as methods of study improved, all theories
were challenged and great scientific discoveries
were made. Men like Galileo, Descartes, Newton,
and Bacon made astonishing advances in the fields
of mathematics, astronomy, philosophy and biology.
Methods of finding dependable knowledge were challenged and tested. Slowly, the older less valid
techniques were discarded.[1] This new emphasis upon
the new scientific process in learning was called
"Realism."

Literature and language became, in realism,
subordinate to scientific and social inquiry. However, special importance was still placed upon moral
education. Many educational theorists felt that time
must be set aside for education in morals to help
balance scientific study. Those who still saw a need
for the use of literature in education were called
humanistic realists.

One of the humanistic realists, Francois Rabelais
(1483-1553), a French monk, physician and scholar saw
a need for secular literature, science and languages
in a ideal education. But he also believed that a
foundation in Christian scriptures was the basis of
morality and strength of character to accompany the
well trained mind.[2]

John Milton (1608-1674), another representative
of humanistic realism, also felt that the development

of moral and responsible character was still important
in this age of scientific inquiry. Cordasco writes
that Milton "objected to the study of mere form and
recommended that the ancient authors be used to teach
science and morality."[3] The moral influence of literature on the education of a scholar, Milton felt,
would help him elucidate scientific ideas and maintain a balance in his education.

> Briefly, Milton advocated a liberal education.
> At school a student would learn science and
> literature and the . . . rules of arithmetic,
> and soon after, the elements of geometry, even
> playing, as the old manner was. After evening
> repast, till bedtime, their thoughts will be
> best taken up in the easy grounds of religion,
> and the story of Scripture.[4]

John Amos Comenius (1592-1670) was born in Mor-
avia in what is now Czechoslovakia. Like Luther,
he rejected the supremacy of the pope and found ultimate authority in the Bible. He became a priest in
the Unity of Brithren, a protestant religion. He was
a prolific writer and very interested in learning
and education.[5]

In his The Great Didactic he poured out his plan
to educate God's children, both boys and girls, in
common schools. He hoped to make learning pleasant
and stressed that coercion in education should be
avoided. Fundamentally, Comenius was first a priest
and thought that education was preparation for eter-
nity. But, he also believed that youth should study
the sciences, arts, and languages to prepare them for
a useful life in this world. He felt that all knowledge could be ordered into meaningful, universal
principles. He found little conflict between the new
inductive methods of science and religion.

The "moral sciences" Comenius talks about were
basically moral virtues such as respect for elders,
justice, temperance in eating and drinking, cleanliness and decorum, and speaking the truth at all times.[6]

There is little that is scientific about Comenius'
moral sciences in the sense of inductive methods
and objectivity but it is of interest to see the
growth of the influence of science and the attempts
of the humanists to reconcile religion, science and
the ancient literature.

Comenius' influence on modern education has been
substantial. Piaget compiled Comenius' writings into
a book and acknowledges being influenced by him. John
Dewey shared Comenius' view that children learn best
when they are actively doing, exploring and imitating.

John Locke (1632-1704), contemporary, was greatly
influenced by Comenius. Locke's philosophical position is empiricist and materialistic. He argued that
experience was an important source of knowledge. However, Locke is often represented as believing that there
are no innate ideas or propensities in the mind. Although it is true that Locke likened the mind to a
blank slate (tabla rasa) or an unmarked waxed tablet,
he acknowledged that children had "Original tempers,"
and that "God has stampd certain Characters upon
Men's Minds, which, like their Shapes, may perhaps
be a little mended; but can hardly be totally altered."[7]

Locke was similar to Rousseau in that he rejected
the notion of the innate depravity of children which
stemmed from original sin. He believed that a good
environment provided by wise parents and an excellent
tutor would help to develop the ability to reason and
to discipline one's self. It should be noted that
Locke's ideas on education were directed exclusively
to the education of the children of the elite. Boys,
especially, should be brought up to understand the
"gentleman's calling."[8]

Perhaps John Locke's most important contributions
to moral education were his ideas concerning the social
contract. He believed that a man enters society with
an implicit agreement that he, the citizen, will turn
over his sovereignty to the government, and the government will in return guarantee protection of the citizen's rights of life, liberty and justice. These

ideas helped build a foundation for statesmen, educators and philosophers to build upon in preparation
for more modern eras. The beginnings of the modern
era will be reviewed in the next chapter.

CHAPTER IX

THE EIGHTEENTH AND NINETEENTH CENTURIES
NEW MOVEMENTS IN EDUCATION

In the 18th and 19th centuries many new concepts were developed in political, economic and intellectual thought which affected the organization and direction of education. The idea and spirit of nationalism was becoming a powerful force and education was viewed as a way to strengthen a sense of nationalism in a population. In addition, the growing middle class of merchants, larger land owners, and industrialists, began to demand education for their children. Later, social reformers and the clergy fought for education for lower class children to protect them from the abuses of child labor in growing industries and to promote literacy and moral education.

Perhaps one of the greatest changes in moral education during this time was the separation of church from state. Almost without exception in the past since the beginning of man's history, education and religion had been combined or at least never consciously separated. Now, Voltaire (1694-1778) said, "no law made by the Church should ever have the least force unless expressly sanctioned by the government."[1] The revolt of the state against the domination of the Church had started earlier with Luther and the German princes and Henry the VIII in Britain. Another Frenchman, La Chalotais (1701-1785) believed that moral education may be needed in the public schools but that the State could direct secular and moral education without Church involvement.[2] About this time Condorcet and others argued that education was necessary for liberty and equality, that education should be universal and include girls and women, that the state should subsidize education, and that the sciences should be included in education.[3]

Jean-Jacques Rosseau (1712-1778) was a romantic naturalist and believed that education and all social institutions except the family were destructive to the innate goodness found in children. Rousseau felt that the advances of technology and science had corrupted society. "Man's true nature" was not being allowed to develop. Proper education included man developing himself by responding to the promptings of the heart and conscience.[4] Rousseau's whole concept of man in his "natural state" revolved around the idea of man's moral goodness and his ability to reason.

> Therefore conscience, which makes us love the one and hate the other, though it is independent of reason, cannot develop without it. . . Before the age of reason we do good or ill without knowing it, and there is no morality in our actions, although there is sometimes in our feeling with regard to other people's actions in relation to ourselves. A child wants to overturn everything he sees. He breaks and smashes everything he can reach; he seizes a bird as he seizes a stone, and strangles it without knowing what he is about.[5]

Nevertheless, Rousseau thought that "the first impulses of nature are always right."[6] Rousseau's theory, as presented in Emile, is an excellent treatise on the moral education of a boy:

> Let us lay it down as an incontestable principle that the first impulses of nature are always right. There is no original perversity in the human heart. Of every vice we can say how it entered and whence it came. The only passion natural to man is self-love, or self-esteem in a broad sense. This self-esteem, has not necessary reference to other people. In so far as it relates to ourselves it is good and useful. It only becomes good or bad in the social application we make of it. Until reason, which is the guide of self-esteem, makes its appearance, the child should not do anything because he is seen or

heard by other people, but only what
nature demands of him. Then he will
do nothing but what is right.[7]

By saying that a child will "do nothing but what
is right," does not mean a child will never do any mis-
chief. Rousseau says, "he might do a great deal that
was bad without being bad, because wrong action depends on harmful intention and that he will never
have."[8] Moral education, to Rousseau, is negative
education. In other words, "it consists not in
teaching virtue and truth, but in preserving the
hear from vice and the mind from error."[9] Again,
like other educators, Rousseau also felt that the
influence of example is paramount in moral education.
"Remember that before you dare undertake the making
of a man," said Rousseau, "you must be a man yourself."[10]

Rousseau's theories influenced many educators.
One who tried to apply Rousseau's theory in education
was (1746-1827) Johann Heinrich Pestalozzi. Much of
Pestalozzi's work laid the foundation of modern elementary education.[11] In his system, moral education
was at the center; he stated:

. . . The final aim of education--humanity--
is only to be reached by subordinating the
demands of our intellectual and practical
capacities to the higher demands of morality
and religion.[12]

Pestalozzi's greatest educational writing was <u>Leonard
and Gertrude</u>, where he emphasized the moral education
of children taught in the home. In this work, which
is a story of the life of a peasant family, the
mother is the primary educator in the home. The
following selection from <u>Leonard and Gertrude</u> helps
to illustrate this point.

Meanwhile, Gertrude had been hurrying
to finish her Saturday's work before Leonard
came back from the Castle. While combing
and braiding the children's hair, mending
their clothes, and putting the room to

rights, she had taught the little ones
a song, with which to greet their father
on his return. As the mason entered,
wife and children stand in chorus:--
"Gentle peace, who art from heaven,
Soothing every pain and care,
Healing with the sweetest balsam
Those who most are in despair,
I am weary of this striving,
I am longing for a rest,--
Higher thou than pain or pleasure,
Come and dwell within my breast!"
"God bless you!" cried Leonard, with
tears in his eyes.
"My dear husband," said Gertrude,
"earth becomes heaven when we seek for
peace, do right, and wish for little."
"If I ever enjoy this heaven on
earth, I owe it to you! I shall thank
you all my life for saving me, and so will
our little ones.--Children, do right, and
follow in your mother's footsteps; then
you will prosper."13

While home was the ideal seat of a child's education, it could only do so much. Schools were
needed to teach subjects which parents could not
teach in the home. Pestalozzi attempted to organize
his schools, however, with a family-like atmosphere.
Pestalozzi said of his school at Stanz:

. . . My first efforts at Stanz were to make
these seventy children feel like brothers
and sisters of a large family, and to make
them affectionate and considerate one towards another.14

Professor John Griscom, manager of a private
school in New York City, made a study of the schools
in Europe in the 1800's. He visited Pestalozzi's
school at Yverdon in 1818 and made these observations:

. . . The children look well, appear very
contented, and apparently live in great

68

harmony one with another; which, considering the diversity of national character and temper here collected, can be attributed only to the spirit of love and affection which sways the breast of the principal of the institution, and extends its benign influence throughout all the departments.

The success of this mode of instruction greatly depends upon the personal qualifications of those who undertake to conduct it. There is nothing of mechanism in it, as in the Lancastrian plan; no laying down of precise rules of managing classes, etc. It is all mind and feeling. Its arrangements must always depend on the ages, talents, and tempers of the scholars, and require on the part of the teachers the most diligent and faithful attention. Above all, it requires that the teacher should consider himself as the father and bosom friend of his pupils, and to be animated with the most affectionate desires for their good. Pestalozzi himself is all this. His heart glows with such a spirit that the good old man can hardly refrain from bestowing kisses on all with whom he is concerned. He holds out his hands to his pupils on every occasion, and they love him as a child loves its mother. His plan of teaching is just fit for the domestic fireside, with a father or mother in the center, and a circle of happy children around them. He is aware of this, and wishes to extend the knowledge of his plan to every parent.[15]

Pestalozzi sought to create a home atmosphere in his schools where students would treat each other with love and consideration.

Pestalozzi's theories in education are a prime example of many educational writers of the 18th-19th centuries in Europe. Many later educational practices in America were transplants from such European models. Many American educators drew upon this European experience and incorporated these into a working model for their own systems.

Immanuel Kant (1724-1804) was a German idealist philosopher. Kant, along with Leibniz and Hegel, other idealists of early modern times, share the optimism in man's free will, the infinite capacity for self-improvement, and the belief that moral laws are absolute.[16] Kant is especially well known for his categorical imperative: "Act only on that maxim whereby thou canst at the same time will that it should become a universal law."[17] Kant's categorical imperative is sometimes compared to Christ's Golden Rule which suggests that we should do unto others as we would have them do unto us. But there is a substantial difference between the two. If an individual follows the Golden Rule he would be obliged to treat others in the same ways that he would like to be treated. If the individual follows Kant's rule, he must consider what would happen if all mankind were to follow his example.

Kant had the optimism characteristic of these early modern realists. He believed that the moral power could be developed through education without compulsion, and that the attractiveness of moral ideas would eventually lead morality to prevail in religion, politics and all phases of human life. All of this depended on faith and a sense of duty.

Kant believed that three great universals were self-existant or eternal ideals. These were: 1) freedom, 2) immortality of the soul, and 3) the existence of God. Freedom is necessary so that moral choices can be made. Immortality of the soul is necessary so that the injustices of this life may be righted. God was viewed by Kant not as person such as Jehovah but the moral forces within man. Moral education either by religion or by schools was important so that the conscience in man could be activated to produce insights which would lead us to do our moral duty and find meaning in mortal life.

Kant disagreed with Rousseau in that he believed that discipline was necessary for children. To encourage a child to follow his impulses without any restraints or discipline could lead a child to become little more than an animal. Our impulses must submit to reason and laws. Kant said of the permissive education of the young princes and princesses of his time:

> It is a common mistake in the education of the great that, because they are destined to rule, they should never meet with opposition in their youth. Owing to his love of freedom, man needs to have his native roughness smoothed down; but with animals instinct renders this unnecessary.[18]

Kant considered education a noble profession for both student and teachers. He thought that mankind had many undeveloped powers, and that discipline and education were necessary so that they could unfold.

> Providence has not placed a fully formed goodness in him, but merely capabilities without moral distinction. Man's duty is to improve himself; to cultivate his mind, and when his is evil, to develop moral character. Upon reflection we shall find this very difficult. Hence education is the greatest and most difficult problem to which man can devote himself.[19]

From this brief exposure to the thinking of Kant one would think that religious leaders of his time would have found him to be a valuable ally. However, Kant didn't believe that church sacraments and dogmas were of much use in attaining salvation or a fully developed moral sense. Further, he saw no need for a divine savior since he didn't believe that man had fallen from grace. He believed that an individual could save himself by harkening to his own moral

71

insights and doing his moral duty. Education and especially moral education were more important to Kant than observance of religious ceremonies.

Perhaps because he never established a demonstration school, Kant's thought hasn't had as much impact on moral education in modern America as has Pestalozzi. But he made important contributions in stressing the importance of education, in stressing the need for discipline, in stressing the importance of doing one's moral duty, and his strong belief in freedom.

CHAPTER X

THE EVOLUTION OF MORAL EDUCATION IN AMERICA

The first American colonists came seeking religious freedom. These Puritans believed that it was important for everyone to be able to read in order that they could read the Scriptures. As a result, schools were established relatively soon after settlement, especially in the New England colonies where settlement patterns in towns made common schools relatively easy to establish. Harvard College was established in 1636 for the training of ministers, a remarkable accomplishment so soon after the founding of the colonies.

Early schools were exclusively religious in nature because the motivation for literacy came from the need to study the Bible and because funds for public schools were probably not available. In the middle and southern colonies, schools were established much more slowly because religions were diverse and because settlement patterns were spread out too much to make schools in towns accessible. Nevertheless, by 1750 almost every town in every colony had passed laws requiring schools even though funds to run schools were often not provided.[1]

Parents were required by law to teach their children to read and write, to study the scriptures, and to be instructed in a trade or skill. If schools weren't available, parents were expected to instruct their children themselves. In practice, the low level of literacy of the parents, especially on the frontier areas, prevented their children from getting much education. Truly widespread and commonly available public schools didn't become common until well into the 1800's.

But the colonists did a remarkably good job of encouraging education and it had a heavy moral emphasis. In addition to the scriptures, the New England Primer was widely used to teach children to read. This

elementary reader discloses the Puritanical attitudes
and religious content in the colonial schools. It
was through the Primer that religious and moral education was taught. The New England Primer contained
pictures and stories which helped children learn the
alphabet. By reciting phrases and seeing pictures
children would learn to read and also learn the
fundamentals of their religious beliefs. For example,
next to the letter "A" is a picture of Adam and Eve
by the fruit tree with the phrase: "In Adam's fall,
we sinned all." Or next to the letter "B" is a picture of the Bible with the phrase: "Thy life to
mend, this book attend." The letter "F" was learned
through "The idle fool, is whipt at school."

The Primer was tremendously influential. It has
been estimated that over 3 million copies were printed
and sold. Millions of early American citizens learned
to read from it and had their views of Christian morality influenced by it.[2]

Other books were published with the same purpose.
They, like the New England Primer, contained cate-
chisms, proverbs, Bible stories, and fables. The following is an example of a fable out of one of these
old time school books, The Universal Spelling-Book.
The title of the fable is "The Town in Danger."

> There was a Town in Danger of being
> besieged, and it consulted which was the
> best Way to fortify and strengthen it;
> and many were the different Opinions of the
> Town Folks concerning it.
> A grave skilful Mason said, there was
> nothing so strong nor so good as Stone.
> A Carpenter said, that Stone might do pretty
> well; but, in his Opinion, good strong Oak
> was much better.
> A currier being present, said, Gentle-
> men, you may do as you please; but to have
> the Town well fortified and secure, take my
> Word, there is nothing like Leather.

'Tis too common for Men to consult
their own private Ends, though a whole
Nation suffer by it.[3]

Each story was carefully placed in these books
so as to develop proper conduct in the students. In
a book called Old Time Schools and Schoolbooks some
excellent examples are given from a wide selection of
books used during the colonial era. Clifton Johnson,
the author of the book mades some excellent observation
about these primers.

The contents of the old-time primers
changed, but for hundreds of years the
teaching of religion and reading continued
united in them. No other way could have been
devised to mould the religious thought of
the people so effectively. The need of
guiding public sentiment on this subject
was plainly apparent; for those who studied
the Bible did not understand its teachings
alike, and printing no sooner gave the
Scriptures a wide distribution than divergent
opinions multiplied. The Bible itself does
not contain a distinct creed, nor does it
tell us what to think about it--hence the
importance of setting forth the simple
tenents of religion in a form for general
distribution. The primers were an especially
valuable medium, because they went to the
fountain head. Their precepts were instilled
in minds as yet unformed, and the children
were drilled to believe what they were to
think out for themselves when they were more
mature.[4]

Examples of how "precepts were instilled" in children's minds could go on and on. The following is a
final example of the precepts children were taught to
believe as they learned to read and spell. This is
taken from The Youth's Instructor in the English Tongue,
Or the Art of Spelling Improved, and called "The
Description of a Good Boy."

The boy that is good
  Does mind his book well;
And if he can't read
  Will strive for to spell.

His school he does love;
  And when he is there,
For plays and for toys,
  No time can he spare.[5]

Many colonial leaders were actively involved in developing American school systems after the Revolution. Benjamin Franklin saw the great need of educating the children of the Revolution. Most of the leaders of the Revolution had been educated in Europe and so when the war was over, a new generation of leaders needed to be educated to carry on. Benjamin Franklin wrote a book--<u>Proposals Relating to the Education of Youth in Pennsylvania</u>, wherein he attempts to define this need and propose a plan to meet that need. His plan involved organizing an Academy where youth could receive a regular education.[6] Franklin saw that a good education was necessary for stability for families and governments. He states:

The good Education of Youth has been esteemed by wise Men in all Ages, as the surest Foundation of the Happiness both of private Families and of Commonwealths. Almost all Governments have therefore made it a principal Object of their Attention, to establish and endow with proper Revenue, such Seminaries of Learning, as might supply the succeeding Age with Men qualified to serve the Publick with Honour to themselves, and to their Country.

Many of the first Settlers of these Provinces, were Men who had received a good Education in Europe, and to their Wisdom and good Management we owe much of our present Prosperity. But their Hands were full, and they could not do all Things. The present Race are not thought to be generally of equal

Ability: For though the American Youth
are allow'd not to want Capacity; yet
the best Capacities require Cultivation,
it being truly with them, as with the
best Ground, which unless well tilled
and sowed with profitable Seed, produces only ranker Weeds.[7]

Morality is one of the subjects he mentions that
must be taught in the proposed Academy and at the end
of his proposal he mentions the "great aim and end of
all learning" is to teach youth to serve mankind,
one's country, friends and family."[8]

The moral education proposed by Franklin centered
around teaching youth to serve man, his country, and
in so doing he could serve God. Those leaders of early
American history all stressed the importance of education in making the new nation stable and strong.
Franklin's proposal was accepted and the first academy
in Pennsylvania was founded. Other similar proposals
helped to form statewide laws to educate the youth.
However, this was not public education. Church groups
established schools and they were not supported with
public money.

Public education got a slow start in America because many felt that moral and religious education
would not be taught in these public schools. Many
church groups felt that these secular schools were non-
Christian and ungodly. The irony of this, however,
is that these church groups actually helped promote
public education.

It was the Sunday School movement which first
promoted the idea of public education. Church groups
would establish schools in poor neighborhoods to teach
rudimentary principles to working children on Sundays
when they weren't working.

Between 1800 and 1825 free school societies were
organized in the larger cities in America to help those
children of the poor for whom no educational opportunities existed.[9] Contrary to the protests from church

groups who said that secular schools were non-Christian and ungodly, public school regulation required that good morals be taught to the youth. Here is what the Report of the Committee for revising the school regulation in Providence, Rhode Island had to say about the teaching of good morals in the school system. This selection was taken from a report written in 1820.

The Publick Schools are established for the general benefit of the community; And all children, of both sexes, having attained the age of six years, shall be received therein and faithfully instructed, without preference or partiality.

The Instruction shall be uniform in the several schools, and shall consist of spelling, Reading, the use of Capital letters and Punctuation, Writing, English Grammar & Arithmetick. . . .

As Discipline and Good Government are absolutely necessary to improvement it is indispensible that the scholars should implicitly obed the Regulations of the Schools.

The good morals of the Youth being essential to their own comfort & to their progress in useful knowledge, they are strictly enjoined to avoid idleness and profaneness, falsehood and deceitfulness, and every other wicked & disgraceful practice; and to conduct themselves in a sober, orderly & decent manner both in & out of school. If any scholar should prove disobedient & refractory, after all reasonable means used by the Preceptor to bring him or her to a just sense of duty, such offender shall be suspended from attendance & instruction in any School, until the next visitation of the committee. Each Scholar shall be punctual in attendance at the appointed hour and be as constant as possible in daily attendance and all excuses for

absence shall be by note, from the Parent
or Guardian of the scholar. . . .
        That they endeavor to impress on
the minds of the scholars a sense of
the Being & Providence of God & their
obligations to love & reverence Him,--
their duty to their parents & preceptors,
the beauty & excellency of truth, justice
& mutual love, tenderness to brute
creatures, the happy tendency of self
government and obedience to the dictates
of reason & religion; the observance
of the Sabbath as a sacred institution,
the duty which they owe to their country
& the necessity of a strict obedience
to its Laws, and that they caution them
against the prevailing vices.[10]

    Many of the public schools were organized to meet
the needs of those children whose parents could not
afford to send them to church sponsored institutions.
Although public schools sought to train children in
moral and religious education, they were criticized by
religious groups who felt that improper doctrine was
being taught to their children. Horace Mann, the great
proponent for public education, sought to tackle this
question head on. Recognizing the importance of moral
education in the schools, he said:

        Moral education is a primal necessity of
social existence. The unrestrained passions
of men are not only homicidal, but suicidal;
and a community without a conscience would
soon extinguish itself.[11]

He also knew that sectarian instruction should be eliminated from the schools and at the same time he
realized that it would not please everyone. In explaining this problem, Mann said:

        In regard to moral instruction, the
condition of our public schools presents
a singular, and, to some extent at least,
an alarming phenomenon. To prevent the
school from being converted into an engine

79

of religious proselytism; to debar successive teachers in the same school,
from successively inculcating hostile
religious creeds, until the children
in their simplemindedness should be
alienated, not only from creeds but
from religion itself; the statute of
1826 specially provided, that no
school books should be used in any of
the public schools "calculated to favor
any particular religious sect or tenet."
The language of the Revised Statutes is
slightly altered, but the sense remains
the same. Probably, no one would desire
a repeal of this law, while the danger
impends it was designed to repel. The
consequence of the enactment, however,
has been, that among the vast libraries
of books, expository of the doctrines of
revealed religion, none have been found,
free from the advocacy of particular
"tenets" or "sects," which includes them
within the scope of the legal prohibition;
or, at least, no such books have been
approved by committees and introduced into
the schools. Independently, therefore,
of the immeasurable importance of moral
teaching, in itself considered, this
entire exclusion of religious teaching,
though justifiable under the circumstances,
enhances and magnifies, a thousand fold,
the indispensableness of moral instruction
and training. Entirely to discard the
inculcation of the great doctrines of
morality and of natural theology has a
vehement tendency to drive mankind into
opposite extremes; to make them devotees
on one side or profligates on the other;
each about equally regardless of the true
constituents of human welfare. Against
a tendency to these fatal extremes, the
beautiful and sublime truths of ethics
and of natural religion have a poising
power.[12]

Mann did not solve this problem but he did define it and bring it into the open for discussion. He also made clear what was needed:

>One of the greatest and most exigent wants of our schools at the present time, is a book, pourtraying, with attractive illustration and with a simplicity adapted to the simplicity of childhood, the obligations arising from social relationships; making them stand out, with the altitude of mountains, above the level of the engrossments of life;--not a book written for the copy right's sake, but one emanating from some comprehension of the benefits of supplying children, at an early age, with simple and elementary notions of right and wrong in feeling and in conduct, so that the appetites and passions, as they spring up in the mind, may, by a natural process, be conformed to the principles, instead of the principles being made to conform to the passions and appetites.[13]

Like Mann, Charles Brooks felt that books were indispensible in teaching moral conduct. Brooks said "that books, like teachers, must have morality in them, else they cannot impart it."[14] "We need books charged with moral electricity," he said, "which will flow by an insensible stream into the student's open soul."[15] Brooks goes on to say that good books which teach moral ideas are essential in education.

>Examine all the school-books used in the public schools of the United States; and you will say that 19 out of 20 go upon the supposition that the intellect only is to be cultivated. You would hardly guess from them, that a child had a heart to be sanctified, as he has a head to be enlightened. I say, then, that we need school-books upon a new plan; books which embrace the whole complex nature of childhood; books which look at the world, at man, at truth and duty,

from God's angle; books which so commun-
icate the divine ideas in science, and
in life, that they can make us think God's
thoughts after him. I see no reason why
we should not have such books; and when
we do have them, what a mighty power will
they become for infusing the eternal principles of Christ's morality into the soul
of inquisitive and impressible childhood.
And this is my third way of teaching morals
in schools.[16]

William McGuffey was one who put this idea to
practice. Like the New England Primer, McGuffey incorporated moral lessons into a book which could be
used in the classroom to teach moral conduct and
build character. It has been estimated that McGuffey
sold more than 100 million copies of his readers
which were used in schoolrooms throughout the nation.[17]
The American McGuffey Society in 1919 claimed that the
McGuffey Reader had the largest circulation in the
world next to the Bible.[18] They also claimed:

William Holmes McGuffey--in his Readers--
furnished the purest English literature ever
collected, anywhere, at any time, each chapter feeding the imagination and the soul of
American youth with the love of home, of
country, of God and mankind, that his days
might be successful and peaceful, and this
Western World might be made better for his
presence therein.[19]

Many lessons were taught in the readers about
honest work, righteous conduct, and duties of the
good Christian citizen. Henry H. Vail, the author
of A History of the McGuffey Readers, talks about
the influence of the reader on students. He said:

From the pages of these readers the
pupils learned to master the printed word
and obtain the thought of the authors.
Without conscious effort they received

moral instruction and incentives toward
right living. Without intent they treas-
ured in their memories such extracts
from the authors of the best English
Literature as gave them a desire to read
more.[20]

While they were learning to read, students also
learned valuable lessons. The following is an example taken from McGuffey's New Fifth Reader. The
title of the selection is "No Excellence Without
Labor."

The education, moral and intellectual,
of every individual, must be, chiefly, his
own work. Rely upon it, that the ancients
were right; both in morals and intellect,
we give the final shape to our characters,
and thus become, emphatically, the archi-
tects of our own fortune. How else could
it happen, that young men, who have had
precisely the same opportunities, should
be continually presenting us with such
different results, and rushing to such
opposite destinies? . . .
And of this be assured, I speak from
observation a certain truth: THERE IS NO
EXCELLENCE WITHOUT GREAT LABOR. It is the
fiat of fate, from which no power of genius
can absolve you.[21]

McGuffey's Readers were used extensively in the
Western and southern part of the United States in
the elementary schools. They were revised four times
after the publication of the First and Second Readers
in 1836. The Third and Fourth Readers were printed
in 1837 with the Fifth and Sixth published in 1844
and 1854, respectively.[22] Each Reader was a little more
difficult than the last with the Sixth Reader being
very sophisticated. Each Reader, however, taught with
the same purpose of developing morals and manners in
children. Notice the moral lesson being taught in this
illustration from McGuffey's New Third Reader:

83

DON'T KILL THE BIRDS

1. DON'T Kill the birds! the
   little birds,
     That sing about your door,
   Soon as the joyous spring has
   come,
     And chilling storms are o'er.

2. The little birds! how sweet
   they sing!
     O, let them joyous live;
   And do not seek to take the
   life,
     Which you can never give.

3. Don't kill the birds! the
   pretty birds,
     That play among the trees;
   For earth would be a cheerless
   place,
     If it were not for these.

4. The little birds! how fond
   they play!
     Do not disturb their sport;
   But let them warble forth their
   songs,
     Till winter cuts them short.

5. Don't kill the birds! the happy
   birds,
     That bless the field and grove;
   So innocent to look upon,
     They claim our warmest love.

6. The happy birds, the tuneful
   birds,
     How pleasant 'tis to see!
   No spot can be a cheerless
   place
     Where e'er their presence be. [23]

At the bottom of this reading was an exercise for the teacher to conduct after the reading. The questions were very thought provoking and no doubt made for a very lively discussion on the morality of killing animals. The questions were:

. . . .--Why should we not kill the birds? Are there not some animals that it is right to kill? What animals, and why?[24,25]

Examples such as these were numerous. The stories and fables in the Readers all taught moral lessons even the famous story "The Boy Who Cried Wolf" is contained in one of the Readers.[26] Many of the selections were taken from the Bible (The Fourth Reader has 17 stories from the Bible), but McGuffey made sure that he would not offend different sects, while at the same time he used religious stories to develop good habits of action and thought.[27] In summing up the influence of the McGuffey Readers we might quote from Vail's work:

. . . No other texts used in the school room bear directly and positively upon the formation of character in the pupils. The school readers are the proper and indispensable texts for teaching true patriotism, integrity, honesty, industry, temperance, courage, politeness, and all other moral and intellectural virtues. In these books every lesson should have a distinct purpose in view and the final aim should be to establish in the pupils high moral principles which are at the foundation of character.[28]

At the turn of the 20th century McGuffey Readers were still being used in many classrooms.

The 19th century has been termed the national period in educational progress and the evolution was from schools funded by religions to universal public schools funded by governments. Inevitably in a diverse and pluralistic society, the public school were obliged to reduce explicit moral education with a religious direction. However, it would be a mistake to assume that moral education disappeared from U.S. public schools. By 1900 moral education had become secular character education which emphasized values common to democracy, and capitalism. The values of hard work, social cooperation, delayed gratification and savings, order and patience, success in life through doing well in school, rational and scientific thought and achievement and success had supplanted the doctrine of original sin and repentence, but moral education still remained in the public schools.

CHAPTER XI

JOHN DEWEY AND MORAL EDUCATION

Although hundreds of religious academies and colleges were established during the 1800's, public schools had become separated from religion by 1900. The separation of church and state that had started in France with Voltaire and Chalotais and continued through our founding fathers through the Constitution had mainly been achieved.

But as increasing numbers of students came to the public schools in the 20th century, it became apparent that simply dispensing information and having students recite was not adequate. Parents sent their children to school because the law requires it, but also because the children were less and less needed at home. In 1776, about 96% of the population was engaged in agriculture in some way. In 1981, less than 5% of the population are farmers. As children had less contact with both parents and churches, many educators made strong pleas for moral education and character education. In 1923, Henry Neuman wrote Education For Moral Growth with a program outlined for the public schools. Programs for character education were outlined by Troth, Hartshorn and May, Jordon, Holmes, Germaine, and others which will be described in more detail in the next chapter.

But John Dewey (1859-1959) is perhaps the most influential philosopher and educator who advocated secular moral education in modern times.

"The work of John Dewey," said Cordasco, an educational historian, "was to formulate a new educational philosophy that challenged both the ends and means of traditional education."[1] Dewey felt that there needed to be a closer relationship between schools and life. He challenged the formalism of the schools of the nineteenth century and advocated an education which involved learning and living. In Dewey's Pedagogic Creed we can understand better what he meant. The following are some excerpts from that creed.

I believe that the school is primarily a social institution. Education being a social process, the school is simply that form of community life in which all those agencies are concentrated that will be most effective in bringing the child to share in the inherited resources of the race, and to use his own powers for social ends. . . . I believe that education, therefore, is a process of living and not a preparation for future living.

I believe that the school must represent present life--life as real and vital to the child as that which he carries on in the home, in the neighborhood, or on the playground.

. . . I believe that it is also a social necessity because the home is the form of social life in which the child has been nurtured and in connection with which he has had his moral training. It is the business of the school to deepen and extend his sense of the values bound up in his home life.

I believe that much of present education fails because it neglects this fundamental principle of the school as a form of community life. . . .

I believe that as such simplified social life, the school life should grow gradually out of the home life; that it should take up and continue the activities with which the child is already familiar in the home.

. . . I believe, finally, that the teacher is engaged, not simply in the training of individuals, but in the formation of the proper social life.

I believe that every teacher should realize the dignity of his calling; that he is a social servant set apart for the maintenance of proper social order and the securing of the right social growth.

> I believe that in this way the teacher
> always is the prophet of the true God
> and the usherer in of the true kingdom
> of God. [2]

In Dewey's theory the home and school helped to train and educate individuals to interact and get along with others in society. The school helped to provide that training. "I believe that the moral education centers upon this conception of the school as a mode of social life," explains Dewey, "that the best and deepest moral training is precisely that which one gets through having to enter into proper relations with others in a unity of work and thought."[3] School was a means of helping others to learn to "Share in the social consciousness"[4] of society. Just as the ideal home should teach the family members to get along with each other and respect each other's rights, the school should do the same for all in a society.

Dewey strongly thought that moral education as a subject could not be directly taught. Teachers couldn't give lessons in moral education because in doing so they would only be saying what others said "about morals." However, teachers do "teach morals" through their actions, through their classroom atmosphere and ideals.[5] Morals could only be learned by interaction with others and not in isolation. Individuals learn moral behavior by testing it and trying it out.

John Dewey's viewpoint on moral education becomes very clear when one closely examines his philosophy in regards to ethics and his philosophy of education.[6] Dewey's main thesis is that there is not a single fixed or final good that can be defined. Instead he maintains that every moral situation is unique having its own unreplaceable good. If Dewey were asked to supply some characteristics of good, he would likely respond with some qualities of mind such as sympathy, sensitivity, persistence, open mindedness, balance of interest, analysis and decision making goals. He believed that the search for the summum bonum or the search for finding rules and fixed ends has produced the controversy that has not allowed for practical application or teaching of ethics. If, in its place, man would search for methods, then practical application would follow; as an individual systematically solves moral dilemmas he develops his moral abilities. Each person has to find a set of rules for good health unique to him. How to live healthily varies with past experiences, opportunity, temperament, inherited weaknesses and strengths. Each person must learn his own way to live healthily and must integrate this aspect of his life with all others.

So it is with moral development. One of Dewey's most adamant claims is that the methods of science have a role in the formation of morals and values. Essential to a science is a knowledge of the relation between changes which enable a person to connect things in terms of antecedents and consequences. He sees no reason why the same procedure cannot be applied to ethics. Dewey frequently argues against a false dichotomy of the world into scientific and non-scientific. This dichotomy results in a disadvantage to our moral knowledge. He maintains that the applications of science to moral questions will eliminate much of what is called subjectivism in regards to moral knowledge. In addition, the application of science to moral questions would show that the principles and standards that seem absolute are in reality only hypotheses and will lose their importance as final causes.

In regards to moral education he argues that education is not a means to an end, but is an end in itself. Education is not preparation for adulthood; learning is not engaged in because it will be useful later on. One does not teach morality because a person needs to be moral later; instead, a person should experience morality in the present. In one breath he equates the educational process with the moral process as a continuous experience of the full range of life. He points out that moral development should be experienced continuously and not viewed as preparation for morality that will occur at a later age. To him morality is independent of age.

Three elements emerged which serve as guides to
Dewey's thinking about moral education. The first
is that morality in the world is still being developed
and there is not one established right, nor will
there ever be. The second states that men by intelligent actions can understand cause and effect and
can shape the direction of the world including the
actions called morality. Third, men's ability to
think about a world in constant change gives rise to
a basic freedom which characterizes the moral efforts
of men.[7]

Dewey was opposed to three main things: (1)
competition for external standing; (2) the passive
inculcation of motives not their own; and (3) remote
success as an end. To clarify the first point, he
takes as an example forty children who were asked to
read from the same books for a certain amount of time.
At the end of that time they were judged relative to
how much they could recall and recite from what they
read. There is not place for individualism. They
are all doing the same thing and should be able to
recall the same thing as the next person.

The social spirit is not cultivated,
in fact, in so far as the purely individualistic method gets in its work, it
atrophies for lack of use. . . . The child
knows perfectly well that the teacher and
all his fellow pupils have exactly the
same facts and ideas before them that he
has; he is not giving them anything at all.
And it may be questioned whether the moral
lack is not as great as the intellectual.
The child is born with a natural desire to
give out, to do, to serve. When this
tendency is not used, when conditions are
such that other motives are substituted,
the accumulation of an influence working
against the social spirit is much larger
than we have any idea of,--especially when
the burden of work, week after week, and
year after year, falls upon this side.[8]

91

Dewey realizes that something must be used to keep the interest of the student on his studies. Often it is an affection or admiration for the teacher, which is fine as far as it goes; but this is purely external and not intrinsic. Because of this it is liable to fade or completely lose its value if external conditions change.

> . . . The child should gradually grow out of this relatively external motive into an appreciation, for its own sake, of the social value of what he has to do, because of its larger relations to life, not pinned down to two or three persons.[9]

The third wrong often committed against children is the use of the remote future as a stimulus for success. Dewey maintains that we often teach children to do things not for the good of doing them, but for the purpose of passing an examination, getting promoted, entering high school, or getting into college.

> Who can reckon up the loss of moral power that arises from the constant impression that nothing is worth doing in itself, but only as a preparation for something else, which in turn is only getting ready for some genuinely serious end beyond.[10]

Dewey points out that the school's primary purpose is to advance the life and welfare of society. His opinion of education is that it is public bussiness and, therefore, the citizens of a community have the right to determine the ultimate goals of a school and also judge the efficacy of the results. This, he feels is the extent and limit to their rights.

The method used to convert the children into the required model citizens should be left to the discretion of the teacher. If the public or their representatives on the boards try to do more than set basic goals, they become mere "meddlers" according to Dewey. He then notes that teaching morality, an effort he acknowledges as essential, must proceed on a social basis. He states: "Apart from participation in social life, the school has no moral end nor aim. As long as we confine ourselves to the school as an isolated institution, we have no directing principles, because we have no object."[11]

> All the rest is mint, anise, and cummin. The one thing needful is that we recognize that moral principles are real in the same sense in which other forces are real; that they are inherent in community life, and in the working structure of the individual. If we can secure a genuine faith in this fact, we shall have secured the condition which alone is necessary to get from our educational system all the effectiveness there is in it. The teacher who operates in this faith will find every subject, every method of instruction, every incident of school life pregnant with moral possibility.[12]

Dewey's thinking about moral education is profoundly different from most of the moral educators of the past. Morality and character for Dewey become "social quality of conduct."[13] Students use the investigative techniques of science in their quest for morals rather than reading scripture or other ancient sacred writings. There is a strong emphasis on action and learning by doing. Schools should not be knowledge factories but experiential and experimental centers for the quest for tested knowledge and values.

Dewey has had a powerful influence on the thinking of several generations of educational thinkers and leaders. But his thought has had less influence on the practices of most public schools. In spite of impressive progressive university laboratory schools and other experimental progressive

schools, most public and private schools have remained
steadfastly essentialist. Elementary schools have
been influenced by Dewey's thought to some degree but
probably more by Pestalozzi, Montessori and others.

Moral education is secular but is still mainly
traditional at both the elementary and secondary
levels. Dewey and his followers such as Theodore
Brameld had hoped that the schools would lead to a
reconstruction of the best in American society. Like
most utopian thought, that hasn't happened yet.

CHAPTER XII

THE TWENTIETH CENTURY: SECULARIZATION IN EDUCATION

As schools became open to the public and tax supported, they could not include religious education, especially a denominational indoctrination, without violating the principle of separation between church and state. The early resolutions were to eliminate denominationalism while professing support of generally Christian virtues and dogma; teaching Christianity without denominationalism required that interpretation be left entirely to the student. However, such a compromise was not acceptable to Catholics and in 1825, Catholics withdrew their children from the public schools in New York City. This seemed to start a general trend towards a more secular content. By the end of the 19th century, with a large immigration of Jews, the public readily welcomed and supported the secularization of the public schools.

In general, two solutions to denominationalism in American public schools evolved: (1) teach a common core of religious beliefs that were shared by all Christian churches, and (2) teach moral and spiritual values apart from any theology. By the 20th century, this latter view had taken precedence. During the early 20th century, a number of programs had been proposed, some even practiced, in which character traits were taught without a demoninational or theological bias. One group, known as the humanists, believed that studying the great works of men would not only refine intellectual abilities but also spiritual faculties. The philosophy of John Dewey lead his advocates to propose that moral and social processes were central to a complete education. A number of organizations such as the International Committee on Moral Instruction and Training in Schools, the Character Development League of New York City, and Character Education Institute were organized for the express purpose of meeting this perceived

deficiency in secular, public schools. Throughout
this century, the National Education Association
has proposed revitalizing the school's curriculum
so that it should include moral and character education. In fact, the tenth yearbook of the Department of Superintendants, National Education Association, was called Character Education and contained numerous proposals for including this aspect
of education in the public schools.[1]

In 1918 the National Education Association
stated seven cardinal principles for secondary education, two of which were citizenship and ethical
character. In 1975 the NEA again issued a reaffirma-
tion of these seven cardinal principles, stating
that ethical character was more important today than
ever before, and that it was an educational imperative.[2,3]

In the 1920's and 1930's, a number of moral or
character education projects were launched. These
early programs were highly directive with specific
goals and ideas; for example, W. W. Charters developed
a program called the teaching of ideals in which certain character traits were to be instilled in students.[4] The program used direct and indirect techniques including use of reward, punishment, and
teacher example. The most ambitious and largest
program was the character education study which ad-
ministered tests to 11,000 pupils between ages of 11
and 16. Their findings were disheartening as they
found no correlation between the students' behavior
and specific training in good moral habits or virtues.[5]

Perhaps the moral education of the early decades
of this century were doomed to fail. There was a
strong public acceptance of the belief in freedom to
choose one's own personal values; and third, there
was diversity among the population of the United
States. No longer did any section of the United
States have a homogeneous population. Disheartened
educators gradually became disenchanted with specific
approaches so that professional and public pressures
for teaching moral behaviors in the schools were

almost nonexistant in the decades preceeding and following World War II.[6]

However, the emotional climate in the late 1960's
and early 1970's again called for some type of moral
education.[7,8] In 1975 the Gallup Poll reported that
up to 85% of parents favored instruction in moral
behavior in the public schools.[9] One research group
surveyed the professional advocacy for moral education and found that during the mid-20th century
most states and state offices of education had recommended some type of instruction that would be classi-
fied as moral, ethical education.[10]

The importance of moral education in the public
schools is also evident in the educational goals
presented by the various states. Of forty-two
State Departments of Education having at least
working drafts of public school educational goals
in 1975, thirty-six (86 percent) had at least one
goal in the moral domain. These goals included such
statements as:

Develops a reasoned commitment to the
values that sustain a free society.
(Connecticut)

Possess an understanding of and respect for himself--his abilities,
interests, values, aspirations, limitations, and uses this understanding
to set personal goals. (Georgia)

Accepts the responsibility of preserving the rights and property of
others. (Georgia)

Clarify his basic values and develop
a commitment to act upon these values
within the framework of his rights and
responsibilities as a participant in
a democratic process. (Washington)

Must foster development of the skills
of creative and critical thinking to
enable students to deal effectively
with situations and problems which
are new to his experience in ways
which encourage him to think and act
in an independent, self-fulfilling
and responsible manner. (Michigan)

To develop an understanding and concern for the rights and needs of
others. (Delaware)[11]

Thus, the advocacy for moral educational content
in the curriculum comes from the public sector, from
professional curriculum specialists, and state governing boards. This pressure has introduced a per-
plexing problem for educational systems attempting
to remain neutral and to separate religion from the
public education. The solutions to this delimma
have taken several forms, and it is to the various
contemporary approaches of moral education in the
public schools that this chapter is addressed.

Contemporary Approaches to Moral Education

Before presenting the various contemporary approaches of moral education, it is well to mention
what is called the hidden curriculum. Essentially,
moral education is thought to be imbedded in all subject matter and extracurricular activities. The
teacher is sometimes asked to highlight moral issues
or themes as they occur in the teaching of literature, art, history, government, etc. In addition,
virtues and values are to be taught through athletics,
band, school government, and vocational education.
Administrators, teachers, and all persons involved
in the educational experience are to be models and
examples--stating their values and opinions in an
indirect fashion. This hidden curriculum has the
value of being non-denominational, and because it is
not formalized and left to the discretion of each
teacher, there is no way to criticize or find fault
with the specific content. Criticisms of the hidden
curriculum focus on its ineffectualness and lack of

openness. If a teacher were to espouse values too strongly or to directly recommend and give moral prescriptions, then the hidden curriculum would no longer be hidden and thus would need to be subject to open public and scholarly scrutiny.

But there is more to the hidden curriculum. Simply by running schools in certain ways values and morals are indirectly modeled. For example, because school administrators and teachers must care for, teach and manage large numbers of students compared to the few children parents have to care for, schools must have many rules. Regular attendance is an important value to administrators because a school loses money (about $10-$15 per day in 1981) each day a student is absent. Punctuality is also important for smooth operation. Obedience, politeness and respect for authority are values that educators appreciate in their students.

In the spring of 1981, Ceinwen King-Smith, a blind Pittsburg high school math teacher was suspended from her job without pay "because her students pelted her with paper balls, tied her shoes together and stole money from her purse."[12] Apparently she is well qualified academically as she graduated Phi Beta Kappa from Stanford University and holds a master's degree from Harvard. She also is experienced as she has 10 years teaching experience.

Without more information it is impossible to make good judgments about this teacher's classroom management skills. But it is very likely that she would have appreciated more empathy from her students and certainly would have liked to have more respect and obedience.

Many critics of education, often academic liberals, have suggested that U.S. public schools are forcing middle class values such as esteem for rational thinking and intellectual skills, sense of accomplishment, honesty, social recognition, cleanliness and self control on all socio-economic classes of students. This is an accurate commentary but a vacuous criticism. If the public schools are to provide an orderly, safe learning environment such middle class values which are part of the hidden curriculum are necessary until alternatives which work are proven. Furthermore, if lower class students are to move into the economic mainstream of American life, most evidence suggests that middle class values, dialects and life styles help to achieve improved economic conditions.

Therefore, it is likely that at least some of the values and morals of the middle class and the Puritan ethic will remain as a part of the hidden curriculum.

Many educators and curriculum specialists have thought that there are basic values that can be identified and upon which both the public and the academic community agree. These basics should be taught to all young people. Within Western governments, these basic elements are usually described as democratic values and include such things as freedom, dignity, justice, equality before the law, self development, etc. While the listings may vary, these educators agree that the process of socialization requires that they be adopted, internalized, and put into action by the time the child reaches adulthood.

Many theoriticians criticize this direct approach to moral education, referring to it as a "bag of virtues." Supposedly, any educational group can simply reach into a "bag of virtues" and select a listing that appeals to them. What is overlooked by these critics is that this is precisely what man has always done and will probably continue to do. It is nearsighted to assume that this is wrong simply because there is variation and differences in the lists selected. For example, one is able to compare various contemporary nations and see the emphasis placed on specific values as a part of national pride and a definition of the nation's culture. Some values are commonly believed to lead to happy, successfully-functioning people. These are elemental values which are shared by a majority of people in society--values such as honesty, integrity, charity, equal opportunity, freedom of speech, patriotism, democracy, and justice, to name but a few. These and similar values have always been incorporated into plans to teach responsible, moral behavior in the schools. Such programs would have the advantage of rejecting "moral neutrality." For example, in a survey of five educational systems, a common concern with moral education emerged. Table 2 contains a list of the primary objectives of the five educational systems.[13]

The instructional methods used to directly teach these basic values generally involves three basic approaches. First, there is the traditional, pedagogical teaching format in which a concept is presented in a classroom situation with illustrations, definitions, and the accompanying testing and evaluation. A second approach related to this method occurs when students are rewarded for demonstrating an understanding and enacting the values being taught. The third method of direct teaching usually involves modeling. As is commonly known, teachers are hired and dismissed on the basis of the example they provide for students. When teachers or students have the "right" values, they are asked to espouse these values and publicly state their opinion. Teachers not holding these values are generally discouraged from mentioning theirs. In addition to teachers, students, community leaders, and national heroes are presented both symbolically and in real life for the purpose of encouraging children to emulate them.

An excellent example of a direct, traditional approach to moral education was developed some years ago by John Wooden, a former basketball coach at U.C.L.A. Wooden was extraordinarily successful winning 7 consecutive national championships and 10 total NCAA championships. Perhaps because Wooden was so successful as a coach, he was able to develop what he calls his "Pyramid of Success." The Pyramid is a classic example of traditional values used to help to win in athletics and to develop character. His values include self control, unselfishness, total dedication, honesty, conditioning of the body, never giving up and many more.[14, 15]

101

TABLE 2

GOALS OF MORAL EDUCATION IN TODAY'S SCHOOLS

Conclusions of a Survey of
Five Educational Systems

United States

Supreme importance of the individual person
Freedom
Common consent as against violence
Devotion to truth
Respect for excellence
Justice and fair play
Brotherhood

Soviet Union

Devotion to communism
Love of work
Dedication to the service of the community
Spirit of internationalism
Intolerance towards injustice and idleness
Deep respect for others
Honesty
Truthfulness
Simplicity
Modesty

Japan

Respect for fellow man
The value of the individual
Democracy
Love of truth
Love of justice
Respect for labour
Responsibility and independence in building a peaceful
  society, domestic and international

TABLE 2 CONTINUED

France

Temperance
Sincerity
Modesty
Kindness
Courage
Tolerance
Love of work
Cooperativeness
Love of country
Sense of duty to family and country
Respect for laws
Generous devotion to the collectivity
Friendship for other peoples
Liberty
Equality
Fraternity

Quebec

Personal responsibility as a man and as a Christian
A Christian ideal for family, professional and social
   life
Freedom
Service of God, Church, fatherland and neighbour
Civic virtues (initiative, respect for law, altruism,
   social awareness, national pride, international
   understanding)
Politeness
Etiquette

SOURCE: D.J. Weeren, Journal of Moral Education, Vol. 2, No. 1, pp. 35-43.

Wooden is a living model of a Christian gentleman and a successful coach. He has credibility! As
a result, many high school coaches, especially in
the West, teach Wooden's moral education as a part of
their coaching.

The direct teaching approach is probably the most
time honored and widely recognized approach to teaching morality. In Appendix A, there are contemporary
programs designed to directly teach values in this
tradition.

Cognitive Development

Here focus is given to a popular psychologist
who has advocated a program for moral education in
the schools. Lawrence Kohlberg has formulated what
he calls a cognitive-developmental theory of moral
reasoning. He follows the tradition of Jean Piaget
and has emphasized the stage aspects of Piaget's
theory. The material for this section is taken primarily from an excellent summary found in the Handbook of Socialization Theory and Research.[16] Kohlberg's six stages are similar to Piaget's theory of
heteronomous and autonomous reasoning. Basically,
Kohlberg's lower three stages are similar to the
heteronomous orientation and the upper three stages
similar to Piaget's autonomous level. Piaget proposed that in the heteronomous stage children are
egocentric and authority bound in their moral reasoning. Through social experience and biological
maturation, the child moves to a higher morality
based on respect of others' needs and viewpoints.
Piaget's theory has generally not stimulated direct
or indirect programs to facilitate moral maturity
or to educate.[17]

Lawrence Kohlberg, on the other hand, has
actively sought to influence educational policy
about moral education. He maintains that levels of
moral maturity can be identified and it is justifiable to try to increase the amount of reasoning at
the higher stages of moral thought. To understand
this argument, it is necessary to present his theory
of moral development.

Table 3 summarizes Kohlberg's classification of moral judgment in stages. The first stage for Kohlberg is a stage where judgments are made on the basis of obedience to commands to avoid punishment. It is deference to authority or power, and persons will be motivated to engage in moral action to avoid punishment.

Stage 2 is an orientation that what is right is defined as what is satisfying to oneself or perhaps the needs of others. For example, moral action would be motivated by a desire to obtain reward for oneself.

Stage 3 is a conformity orientation where one engages in actions to gain the approval or please others.

Stage 4 is orientation direction towards doing one's duty or being obedient to law. The essence of this morality is showing respect for authority and maintaining the social order. Actions are evaluated in terms of institutional order or duty.

Stage 5 is a moral social contract orientation. There is a recognition that rules exist by mutual or common consent. Generally institutions are justified in terms of humanitarian of human welfare. One's moral actions are motivated for maintaining community and individual well-being recognizing the social basis for law and institutions. An individual at this level of moral reasoning must have true formal thought (hypo-dedective, multiple causation thinking as per Piaget), and understand the spirit as well as the letter of the law such as in the U.S. Constitution.

Stage 6 is called conscience or universal ethical principle orientation. Social rules are those subdivided by adherence by the principles of choice resulting from logical analysis and basic principle of conscience. Individual appraisal is a guiding principle based on mutual respect and trust. Basically, Kohlberg emphasized the concept of justice at this stage. One engages in moral actions to avoid self-condemnation or violating ones own principles; i.e., he is more concerned about his self-respect than the community's respect, as in level 5 or 4.[18]

Since 1976, Kohlberg has decided that Stage 6 is more accurately a sub-stage of Stage 5 and is more an ideal attained by a tiny minority rather than a universal stage. So in recent writings by and about Kohlberg, Stage 5b replaces Stage 6.[19]

Kohlberg developed these stages after analyzing the results of interviews, in which he presented moral dilemmas to adolescent boys and asked them their opinions requiring moral reasoning. In order for the readers to gain a more thorough understanding of these dilemmas, the following story is presented.

In Europe, a woman was near death from cancer. One drug might save her, a form of radium that a druggist in the same town has recently discovered. The druggist was charging $2,000, ten times what the drug cost him to make. The sick woman's husband, Heinz, went to every one he knew to borrow the money, but he could only get together about half of what it cost. He told the druggist that his wife was dying and asked to sell it cheaper or let him pay later. But the druggist said, "no." The husband got desperate and broke into the man's store to steal the drug for his wife. Should the husband have done that? Why?[20]

According to Kohlberg, you could answer "yes" or "no" to the question and justify your answers with any of the reasoning from any of the six stages.

The role of social experience in producing the moral level is regarded by Kohlberg as important. He says that if the person is given an appropriate opportunity for action and can reflect on a given stage of reasoning when his mind is at the same structural development, then it would be predicted that he would prefer and use the stated level of moral reasoning.

The value of cognitive development is dependent on the assumption that one who reasons more maturely also behaves more maturely. Kohlberg is aware of this assumption and asserts that under favorable conditions there may be an integration of moral thought and action.

Educators and program developers who follow Kohlberg's model generally assume that the movement toward higher levels of moral reasoning will occur naturally if the person is allowed to freely interact and discuss moral problems in a healthy environment. Accordingly, the instructional methodology proposed is to present moral dilemmas, as the one described earlier, and then to encourage reaction, reasoning, and reflection on the dilemma.

Although Kohlberg's theory has created much enthusiasm among theorists and practitioners, the effectiveness of Kohlberg's moral education is still in question. The theory is certainly heuristic. But anthropologists, educators and psychologists have raised questions about its universality, the reality of Stage 6, its measureability, and its effectiveness in raising cognitive moral reasoning. For example, Nichols did a longitudinal study for 3 years with junior high school students in Minnesota. He found few differences in the moral reasoning of students exposed to a Kohlberg social studies curriculum compared to a control group following a traditional history curriculum. Most of the changes in the students were attributable to maturation as much as any intervention.[21]

But even with its limitations, Kohlberg's theory should be taken seriously. Part of its appeal may stem from the non-relative firm value base. In the Kohlberg stages, each successive stage is more unselfish and altruistic than the stage below it.

TABLE 3

CLASSIFICATION OF MORAL JUDGMENT INTO
LEVELS AND STAGES OF DEVELOPMENT

Level	Basis of Moral Judgment	Stage of Development
I	Moral values reside in external, quasi-physical happenings, in bad acts, or in quasi-physical needs rather than in person and standards.	Stage 1: Obedience and punishment orientation. Egocentric deference to superior power or prestige, or a trouble-avoiding set. Objective responsibility. Stage 2: Naively egoistic orientation. Right action is that instrumentally satisfying the self's needs and perspective. Naive egalitarianism and orientation to exchange and reciprocity.
II	Moral value resides in performing good or right roles, in maintaining the conventional order and the expectancies of others.	Stage 3: Good-boy orientation. Orientation to approval and to pleasing and helping others. Conformity to stereotypical images of majority or natural role behavior, and judgment by intentions.

TABLE 3 CONTINUED

		Stage 4: Authority and social-order maintaining orientation. Orientation to "doing duty" and to showing respect for authority and maintaining the given social order for its own sake. Regard for earned expectations of others.
III	Moral value resides in conformity by the self to shared or shareable standards, rights or duties.	Stage 5: Contractual legalistic orientation. Recognition of an arbitrary element or starting point in rules or expectations for the sake of agreement. Duty defined in terms of contract, general avoidance of violation of the will or rights of others, and majority will and welfare.
		Stage 6: Conscience or principle orientation. Orientation not only to actually ordained social rules but to principles of choice involving appeal to logical universality and consistency. Orientation to conscience as a directing agent and to mutual respect and trust.

TABLE 3 CONTINUED

SOURCE: Adapted from: L. Kohlberg, "Moral Stages and Moralization," in T. Lichona, ed., Moral Development and Behavior: Theory, Research, and Social Issues (New York: Holt, Rinehart, & Winston, 1976), pp. 31-53.

Kohlberg's stages bear some resemblance to the ideal-
ism of Kant and Leibnitz in that there is an underlying optimism about human nature and some absolutes
exist. Perhaps Socrates would find some aspects of
Kohlberg's theory congenial too.

From the practitioner's point of view, many curriculum materials have been developed for use with
junior and senior high school students. Specific
programs based on Kohlberg's ideas are presented in
Appendix B.

Social Science Education

It appears that curriculum specialists in social
science have produced one of the more unique and
interesting approaches to moral education. The approach could be called applied axiology using logical
thinking and procedures of science to deal with
values and moral problems. In this approach students
learn to provide facts about whether something is
good or of value. The student must justify his statements. Feelings and passions are put secondary to
the acquisition of a rational approach to morality.

Because social science specialists have developed
these approaches, the instruction generally involves
learning to handle social hypothetical problems,
issues, and questions. Ordinarily, the method employed is group study, library and field research,
and class discussion. To explain this approach, the
following sequence of steps was condensed from the
41st yearbook of the National Council for the Social
Studies.

1. Identify and clarify the value questions:
    Clarify by defining terms from which the
    evaluation is to be made. Specify the value
    object to be judged.

2. Assemble facts: Gather and organize facts to
    make a value judgment.

111

3. Assess the truth of facts: Assess the truth of purported factual assertions by finding supporting evidence and by assessing the source of the purported fact.

4. Clarify the relevance of facts: Clarify the relevance of the facts by encouraging and insuring that a) the facts are about the value object in question; and b) the evaluator has criteria which gives the facts a positive or negative balance.

5. Arrive at a tentative value decision: Decide tentatively the answer to the value question.

6. Test the value principle implied in the decision: Test the value principle implied in their decision for acceptability in any of the following four ways. a) New cases test: formulate the value principle explicitly, imagine other situations in which it would logically apply, and decide if one can accept its application in these situations. b) Subsumption test: formulate the value principle explicitly and assemble facts (evidence) that show that the value principle is a case of some more general value principle that the evaluator accepts. c) Role exchange test: imaginatively exchange roles with someone else affected by the application of the value principle and consider whether he or she can still accept the principle as it applies to him or her in this role. d) Universal consequences test: imagine what the consequences would be if everyone in similar circumstances were to engage in the action being evaluated and consider whether one can accept these consequences.[22]

Jurisprudential/Analysis of Public Issues

An approach to values education that is similar to the Social Science Education approach but is much more fully developed in terms of its rationale and curriculum materials is James P. Shaver's jurisprudential approach. An elaborate curriculum package

112

is published by Houghton Mifflin as the Analysis of Public Issues Program. A very detailed instructors' manual is provided. Students have a text entitled Decision Making in a Democracy and there are problem booklets and a media package.[23]

Shaver and Larkins believe that the primary purpose of social studies is to develop citizenship skills. The fundamental value of our pluralistic democracy is the dignity of the individual. Every decision a citizen makes should be weighed against the inherent value and dignity of the individual.

Students can prepare for responsible adult citizenship by practicing making decisions about public issues in their social studies classrooms. Students should learn to identify problems, propose possible solutions, explore consequences, identify values that conflict and try to resolve the conflict by referring to a higher level value, gather and evaluate data, and come to a qualified decision.

The Analysis of Public Issues Program is neo-progressive in that there is a strong emphasis on the need for teachers to develop a thoughtful rationale for teaching, there is an emphasis on inquiry process skills, and a strong commitment to democratic values.

In the judgment of the junior author, it is unfortunate that this program hasn't been more widely used because it is excellent in many dimensions. Its main limitation may be that it is difficult for both teacher and students. Only a teacher who is well informed and is a skillful discussion leader can do justice to this program.

Additional information and references are available in Appendix C.

Values Clarification

The following quote illustrates the approach described in this section.

We are interested in the processes that are going on. We are not much interested in identifying the values which children believe that in a world that is changing as rapidly as ours, each child must develop habits of examining his purposes, aspirations, attitudes, feelings, etc., if he is to find the most intelligent relationship between his life and the surrounding world, and if he is to make a contribution to the creation of a better world: . . . The development of values is a personal and life-long process. It is not something that is completed by early adulthood.[24]

These authors, Louis Raths, Merrill Harmin, and Sidney Simon advocate teaching valuing rather than teaching ancient, traditional, or ever recently derived values to youth. They proposed to teach children better ways to value (value used as a verb).

The major goal proposed in this model is to develop a person capable of valuing. What does valuing mean? The authors propose that there are seven basic elements which will characterize a person who is valuing. They are:

1. Choosing freely. If something is in fact to guide one's life whether or not authority is watching, it must be a result of free choice. If there is coercion, the result is not likely to stay with one for long, especially when out of the range of the source of that coercion. Values must be freely selected if they are to be really valued by the individual.

2. Choosing from among alternatives. This definition of values is concerned with things that are chosen by the individual and, obviously, there can be no choice if there are no alternatives from which to choose. It makes no sense, for example, to say that one values eating. One really has no choice in

the matter. What one may value is certain types of food or certain forms of eating, but not eating itself. We must all obtain nourishment to exist; there is no room for decision. Only when a choice is possible, when there is more than one alternative from which to choose, do we say a value can result.

3. Choosing after thoughtful consideration of the consequences of each alternative. Impulsive or thoughtless choices do not lead to values as we define them. For something intelligently and meaningfully to guide one's life, it must emerge from a weighing and an understanding. Only when the consequences of each of the alternatives are clearly understood can one make intelligent choices. There is an important cognitive factor here. A value can emerge only with thoughtful consideration of the range of the alternatives and consequences in a choice.

4. Prizing and cherishing. When we value something, it has a positive tone. We prize it, cherish it, esteem it, respect it, hold it dear. We are happy with our values. A choice, even when we have made it freely and thoughtfully, may be a choice we are not happy to make. We may choose to fight in a war, but be sorry circumstances make that choice reasonable. In our definition, values flow from choices that we are glad to make. We prize and cherish the guides to life that we call values.

5. Affirming. When we have chosen something freely, after consideration of the alternatives, and when we are proud of our choice, glad to be associated with it, we are likely to affirm that choice when asked about it. We are willing to publicly affirm our values. We may even be willing to champion them. If we are ashamed of a choice, if we would not

make our position known when appropriately asked, we would not be dealing with values but something else.

6. Acting upon choices. Where we have a value, it shows up in aspects of our living. We may do some reading about things we value. We are likely to form friendships or to be in organizations in ways that nourish our values. We may spend money on a choice we value. We budget time or energy for our values. In short, for a value to be present, life itself must be affected. Nothing can be a value that does not, in fact, give direction to actual living. The person who talks about something but never does anything about it is dealing with something other than a value.

7. Repeating. Where something reaches the stage of a value, it is very likely to reappear on a number of occasions in the life of the person who holds it. It shows up in several different situations, at several different times. We would not think of something that appeared once in a life and never again as a value. Values tend to have a persistency, tends to make a pattern in a life.[25]

They are able to distinguish between the process of valuing or a value according to the following: (1) goals or purposes, (2) aspirations, (3) attitudes, (4) interests, (5) feelings, (6) beliefs and convictions, (7) activities, and (8) worries and problems. Each of these eight listed human activities is similar to a value in one way or another, but still is not a value. All are related or indicators of valuing and are benefited by an improvement in the processing of valuing.

Comprehensive and detailed instructional materials have been developed for teaching value clarification. The essentials of these specific techniques are outlined below.

116

1. Encourage children to make choices, and
   to make them freely.

2. Help them discover and examine available
   alternatives when faced with choices.

3. Help children weigh alternatives thoughtfully, reflecting on the consequences of
   each.

4. Encourage children to consider what it is
   that they prize and cherish.

5. Give them opportunities to make public
   accordance with their choices.

6. Encourage them to act, behave, live in
   accordance with their choices.

7. Help them to examine repeated behaviors
   or patterns in their life.[26]

   The purpose of these techniques is to raise
questions in the minds of children to help them
examine basic issues, actions, and ideas. Basically,
it is an attempt to help the children examine their
lives and to think about it in a climate of positive
acceptance and intelligence. A certain interpersonal
atmosphere of trust and respect is essential. It is
usually done on an informal, face to face, personal
basis. The basic accomplishment is that it shifts
the responsibility of values from the teacher to the
students who must do the examination and valuing.
Generally, it is not mechanical, and there are few
if any theoretically right or wrong answers.

   This approach has basically been derived from
the humanistic theories of psychology prevalent and
developed during the mid-20th century. Here, internal
rather than external factors are deemed to be the
prime motivators of human behavior. By changing a
person's values, behavior is free to change and will
inevitably change; but one must carefully understand

and work through his or her values. This approach
has become one of the most widespread and extremely
controversial methods of vlaue education. Materials
have proliferated and some of the more basic materials are presented in Appendix D.

Summary

     The 20th century began by building upon the
writing of John Dewey. Shortly after Dewey had become a mentor of many United States educators, a
large number of programs intending to directly
teach moral education emerged. These were usually
concerned with teaching basic values, traditional
ethics, and democratic principles. They generally
met with public favor, support from school boards,
and state educational agencies. However, they
never flourished or became a central part of education in the United States. In fact, they diminished
in importance, and until in the years immediately
following World War II there were few noticeable
attempts to teach morals, ethics, or values in the
public schools.

     Those acquainted with education in the United
States will note that it is during these years
especially after 1957, that a strong emphasis was
placed on the sciences primarily for the purpose
of national defense and maintaining world leadership
in science and technology.

     However, judging by public opinion polls and
educators' interest, a new concern regarding the
values and ethics of the citizens has emerged during
the sixties and seventies; and at the present time,
there are several popular approaches to moral education. However, most of these approaches are only in
their infancy of curriculum development.

     The first approach is the hidden curriculum
with no specific content. The second approach is
a series of programs basically involving traditional
values and direct instruction, reward for appropriate

behavior, and modeling. The third is Kohlberg's cognitive approach which is speculative and a theoretical model designed to help facilitate the moral thinking of an individual. Other approaches include curriculum developed by social studies specialists, applying a philosophy of axiology to moral situations. Generally they seek to develop scientific or rational skills for solving moral problems. An especially well developed program of this type is Shaver's and Larkins' <u>Analysis of Public Issues Program</u>. The last approach described is value clarification based on a humanistic understanding of man. Essentially, the student acquires skill in learning to clarify the values he has.

With the exception of the direct teaching approaches, the reader might note that educators and curriculum specialists show considerable timidity in proposing any solid content for moral education in the 20th century. Note that in several of the approaches, no absolute values are proposed by these theories. Most of the approaches primarily teach a skill or a process rather than specific content.

EPILOGUE

After reviewing the mainstream of Western education for over 2,000 years, it is clear that morality has been a central concern in education. To
educators and critics who attack the introduction of
moral content into the contemporary educational
offerings, the nearsightedness of their objections
is obvious when considering the historical perspective. Only in recent years in the United States have
educators attempted to provide an education without
a clear moral content. The basis for eliminating
moral content from the curriculum are: 1) a need for
a separation of church and state, and 2) respect for
individuality. These two values, while important
and fundamental, raise fears about introducing moral
content in the curriculum; but they are not an adequate argument for its elimination.

It is clear that there will not be a dominant
religion in the United States, and hence fear of
widespread religious indoctrination is unfounded in
reality. The second concern with respect to man's
individuality does not require that moral content
must be eliminated from the curriculum. Even when
there has been a common core of morality, men have
differed. In addition, there are certainly instructional programs available which will allow individuality. Furthermore, if individuality is desired and
universally accepted, then this value of individuality can be proposed and become a part of the content.

The basic concern with indoctrination is a
relatively new phenomenon: in previous centuries
homogeneous cultures felt free to directly indoctri-
nate youth in the prevailing values and beliefs
system. Today, this is not so and thus, there is a
general fear; the fear of either being indoctrinated
or indoctrinating others. It would appear that the
fears of separation of church and state, the loss of
uniqueness in moral perspective, and the possibility
of indoctrinating persons against their will are
contemporary concerns which form the basis of most

121

objections to moral eduation in the schools. These
fears have probably been responsible for the lack of
moral content in the curriculum. However, three of
the popular moral education programs today circumvent
these fears by focusing only on the processes of
thinking, valuing, and reasoning. If a person is
taught to think about moral issues, to become more
mature in his moral concepts, and to reason or value,
then he certainly could not be said to have been
indoctrinated, to have been immersed in a one-sided,
theological perspective, or to have his individuality
and uniqueness of moral perspective threatened.

However, by focusing only on the processes, it
may not be possible to meet the demands of a public
and of state agencies as well as professional curriculum planners who desire to have moral conduct
strengthened through school attendance. For example,
a predominant concern of parents about public schools
is discipline. They are also frightened about drugs,
violence, and declining standards. At this writing
there is little reason to believe that process oriented moral education will solve the serious problems
in public schools. To be fair, direct traditional
moral education would probably not solve our serious
educational problems either.

If public schools, especially in large cities,
continue to deteriorate, private schools will grow--
especially if the Federal government grants tax
credits or makes vouchers available for use in private schools. It is a reasonable prediction that
moral education in private schools will be content
oriented and will often be clearly religious as in
Catholic parochial schools.

In regards to moral education, the public schools
are facing a difficult dilemma. Stanley F. Bonner
described the difficulties of education in a decadent
society in his recent book on Education in Ancient
Rome. Most of us prefer not to view the United
States as decadent or sick. But our sensibilities
are hammered too frequently by assassination attempts,
terrorism, violence in our cities and schools, and

122

confusion about what we stand for and value as a nation. We have done well in accommodating much pluralism and diversity in lifestyle and belief systems. Our record is not as good in extending equal opportunity to all and in lifting up the underclass.

Perhaps we will have to find a unifying focus and purpose as a nation as described by Durkheim[2] in order for the schools to have a clear mandate about moral education. Perhaps we are at a turning point in history when a new synthesis of content and inquiry process may emerge. The challenge is before and very real.

FOOTNOTES

CHAPTER I. UNDERSTANDING MORAL PERSPECTIVES

[1]Marie Ossowaska, Social Determinants of Moral Ideas (Philadelphia: University of Pennsylvania Press, 1970) p. 109.

[2]Herbert Barry, Irvin Child, Margaret Bacon, "The Relations of Child Training to Subsistance Economy," American Anthropologist (61, 1959) 61-63.

[3]Daniel R. Miller, Guy E. Swanson, Inner Conflict of Defense (New York: Holt, Rinehart & Winston, 1958).

[4]Eric Fromm, The Sane Society (New York: Holt, Rinehart & Winston, 1955).

[5]Boyd McCandless, Children's Behavior and Development (2nd Ed. New York: Holt, Rinehart & Winston, 1976), pp. 584-594.

[6]Daniel Yankelovich, The New Morality: A Profile of American Youth in the Seventies (New York: McGraw-Hill, 1974).

[7]William Lambert, Leigh Minturn Triandis, Margery Wolf, "Some Correlations of Beliefs in the Malovolence of Supernatural Beings: A Cross-societal Study," Journal of Abnormal and Social Psychology (58, 1959), pp. 162-169.

[8]Richard T. Degeorge, Soviet Ethics in Morality Ann Arbor: University of Michigan Press, 1969.

[9]Urie Bronfenbrenner, "Soviet Methods of Character Education: Some Implications for Research," American Psychologist (17, 1962), pp. 550-564.

[10]Robert Sundley, "Early Nineteenth-Century American Literature on Child-Rearing," cited in E.D. Evan's Children's Reading in Behavior and Development (New York: Holt, Rinehart & Winston, 1968, 13).

125

FOOTNOTES (Continued)

CHAPTER I

[11]Sidney Jourard, Healthy Personality, And Approach from the Viewpoint of Humanistic Psychology (New York: MacMillan, 1974).

FOOTNOTES

CHAPTER II.   A COMPARISON BETWEEN A
PRIMITIVE SOCIETY AND MODERN AMERICA

[1] Dorothy Rogers, _Adulthood and Aging_ (Englewood Cliffs: Prentice Hall, 1979).

[2] "95 pct. Call Themselves Religious," _Desert News_. March 25, 1977, p.23.

[3] Richard Borshay Lee, _The ! Kung San: Men, Women and Work in a Foraging Society_ (New York: The Cambridge University Press, 1979).

[4] George Gallup, "Americans Favoring Return to Normalcy," _The Salt Lake Tribune_ June 22, 1978, p.A5.

[5] William Hillcourt, _Official Boy Scout Handbook_ (Irving, TX: Boy Scouts of America, 1979).

[6] James C. Coleman et al. _Equality of Educational Opportunity_ (Washington, D.C. U.S. Government Printing Office, 1966).

[7] Elizabeth T. Marshall, _The Harmless People_ (New York: Alfred A. Knopf, 1959).

[8] Lee, _The ! Kung San_, pp. 370-400.

[9] Ibid., pp. 250-308.

CHAPTER III.   JEWISH AND EARLY
CHRISTIAN MORAL EDUCATION

[1]"95 pct. "Call Themselves Religious," Desert News,
p.23.

[2]Gallup, The Salt Lake Tribune, p. A5.

[3]THE BIBLE: A New English Translation (Oxford:
Oxford and Cambridge University Presses, 1970), pp. 82-83

[4]The Living TALMUD: The Wisdom of the Fathers
(New York: Mentor, 1957), pp. 26-27.

[5]Joseph Campbell, The Masks of God: Occidental
Mythology (New York, Penguin Books, 1964), pp. 125-126.

[6]THE BIBLE: King James Version. (Oxford: 1951),
pp. 7.

[7]Ibid., p. 8.

[8]Adolph E. Meyer, An Educational History of the
Western World (New York: McGraw-Hill, 1965), pp. 63-66.

CHAPTER IV.   A STUDY OF ANCIENTS--
GREEK AND ROMAN EDUCATION

[1]Paul Monroe, ed., Source Book of the History
of Education for the Greek and Roman Period (New
York: The Macmillan Co, 1901), p. 2.

[2]Charles F. Arrowood and Frederick Eby, The
History and Philosophy of Education, Ancient and
Medieval (New York: Prentice-Hall, 1940),

[3]Ibid., p. 194.

[4]Hugh C. Black et al., The Great Educators Readings for Leaders In Education. (Chicago: Nelson-Hall
Co. 1972), p. 180.

[5]Fredrick Mayer, A History of Educational Thought
(Columbus: Charles E. Merrill, 1966), pp. 90-95.

[6]Ibid., p. 91.

[7]Francesco Cordasco, A Brief History of Education
(Totowa, New Jersey: Littlefield, Adams and Co., 1967),
pp. 6-7.

[8]Robert D. Cummings, ed., Plato: Euthyphro,
Apology; Crito (New York: The Liberal Arts Press,
1956), pp. 44-45.

[9]Francis M. Cornford, ed., The Republic of
Plato (London: Oxford University Press, 1957), p. 70.

[10]Taken from a selection of Plato's Republic
quoted in R. L. Nettleship's The Theory of Education
in Plato's Republic (London: Oxford University Press,
1955), p. 33.

[11]Nettleship, Theory of Education in Plato's
Republic, p. 42.

[12]Taken from Book II of Plato's Republic quoted
in Monroe's Source Book, p. 139.

CHAPTER IV.   (continued)

[13]Taken from a selection of Aristotle's _Politics_ quoted in Monroe's _Source Book_, p. 281.

[14]Ibid., p. 280.

[15]Ibid., p. 282.

[16]Taken from a selection of Aristotle's _Ethica Nicomachea_ quoted in Arrowood and Eby's _History and Philosophy of Education_, p. 428.

[17]Ibid., p. 429.

[18]Ibid., p. 430.

[19]Cordasco, _Brief History of Education_, pp. 9-10.

[20]Monroe, _Source Book_, p. 425.

[21]Black, _The Great Educators_, p. 203-204.

[22]Stanley F. Bonner, _Education In Ancient Rome_ (Berkeley: U. of California Press, Berkeley, 1979).

[23]Fredrick M. Binder, _Education in the History of Western Civilization: Selected Readings_ (New York: MacMillan, 1970), p. 43.

[24]Bonner, _Education In Ancient Rome_, p. 104.

[25]Mayer, _A History of Educational Thought_, p. 121.

[26]Emile Durkheim, _Moral Education_ (New York: The Free Press of Glencoe, 1961), pp. 12-14.

CHAPTER V.   CHRISTIAN EDUCATION
IN THE EARLY MIDDLE AGES

[1]Rev. Frederick Crombie, trans., The Writings of Origen (London: Hamilton and Co., 1869), p. 184.

[2]Ellwood P. Cubberly, Readings in the History of Education. N.Y., 1920 p. 77.

[3]Ibid., p. 90.

[4]Ibid., p. 106.

[5]Kendig B. Cully, Basic Writings in Christian Education, (Philadelphia: Westminister Press, 1960), pp. 96-97.

[6]Paul Abelson, The Seven Liberal Arts: A Study in Medieval Culture (New York: Teachers College, Columbia University, 1906; reprint ed., New York: Russel and Russel, Inc., 1965), pp. 14-15.

[7]Manuel Komroff, ed., The Tales of the Monks from the Gesta Romanorum, trans. Rev. Charles Swans (New York: Tudor Publishing, 1936), p. xi.

[8]Ibid., pp. 29-30.

[9]Kendig B. Cully, Basic Writings in Christian Education (Philadelphia: Westminster Press, 1960), pp. 95-96.

[10]Edward J. Power, Main Currents in the History of Education (New York: McGraw-Hill, 1970), p. 304.

[11]Percival R. Cole, A History of Educational Thought (Oxford University Press, 1931), p. 156.

[12]Lynn Thorndike, University Records and Life in the Middle Ages (New York: Columbia University Press, 1944), p. 30.

CHAPTER V.   (continued)

[13]Ibid, pp. 26-27.

[14]Cubberly, _Readings_, p. 125.

[15]Ibid., pp. 175-176.

[16]Ralph L. Pounds, _The Development of Educational Thought_ (New York: Appleton-Century-Crofts, 1968), p. 142.

CHAPTER VI.   THE RENAISSANCE--A
RENEWED INTEREST IN CLASSICAL THOUGHT

[1]Power, Main Currents, p. 293.

[2]Desiderius Erasmus, The Education of a Christian
Prince, trans. Lester K. Born (New York: Columbia
University Press, 1936), p. 141.

[3]Ibid., p. 141.

[4]Desiderius Erasmus, Concerning the Aim and
Method of Education, trans. and ed. William H. Woodward
(New York: Teachers College, Columbia University,
1904), pp. 184-185.

[5]Erasmus, Education of Christian Prince, p. 146.

[6]Clara P. McMahon, Education in Fifteenth-Century
England (New York: Greenwood Press, 1968), p. 142.

CHAPTER VII.   REFORMATION--THE MORAL
AND RELIGIOUS EDUCATIONAL THEORIES OF LUTHER

[1]H.G. Wells, The Outline of History (New York:
Garden City Books), 1961, p. 631.

[2]Frederick Eby, Early Protestant Educators: The
Educational Writings of Martin Luther, John Calvin,
and Other Leaders of Protestant Thought (New York:
McGraw-Hill, 1931), p. 5.

[3]Ibid., p. 24.

[4]Ibid., pp. 30-31.

[5]Ibid., pp. 80-81.

[6]Ibid., pp. 35-43.

CHAPTER VIII.   REALISM: A SCIENTIFIC AND
PHILOSOPHICAL APPROACH TO EDUCATION

[1]Power, Main Currents, pp. 329-363.

[2]Cubberly, Readings, p. 331.

[3]Cordasco, Brief History of Education, p. 63.

[4]Oliver M. Ainsworth, ed., John Milton, The
Tractate of Education, (New Haven: Yale University
Press, 1928), pp. 55, 57.

[5]Power, Main Currents, pp. 339-341.

[6]Jean Piaget, ed., John Amos Comenius Selections
(Switzerland: Unesco, 1957), p. 22.

[7]Hugh C. Black and others, The Great Educators:
Readings for Leaders in Education.   Education of
the Gentry.   pp. 434.

[8]Ibid., p. 437-438.

CHAPTER IX.   THE EIGHTEENTH - NINETEENTH CENTURIES
NEW MOVEMENTS IN EDUCATION

[1]Cubberly, Readings, p. 395.

[2]Ibid., pp. 410-411.

[3]Cordasco, Brief History of Education, p. 80.

[4]Ibid., p. 81.

[5]Jean Jacques Rousseau, Emile: Selections, trans.
and ed. William Boyd (New York; Teachers College, Columbia
Univ., 1962), p. 39.

[6]Ibid., p. 40.

[7]Ibid., p. 40.

[8]Ibid., p. 40.

[9]Ibid., p. 41.

[10]Ibid., p. 42.

[11]Cordasco, Brief History of Education, p. 89.

[12]John A. Green, The Educational Ideas of
Pestalozzi (New York: Greenwood, Press, 1969), p. 131.

[13]Pestalozzi, Leonard & Gertrude (Boston: D.C.
Heath and Co., 1891), p. 19.

[14]Green, Educational Ideas of Pestalozzi, p. 139.

[15]Binder, Education in the History of Western
Civilization, pp. 300-304.

[16]Mayer, A History of Educational Thought,
pp. 268-276.

CHAPTER IX. (continued)

[17]Ibid., p. 271.

[18]Ibid., p. 274.

[19]Ibid., p. 275.

CHAPTER X. EVOLUTION OF MORAL
EDUCATION IN AMERICA

[1]Cubberly, Readings, pp. 306-307.

[2]Ibid., pp. 303-315.

[3]Clifton Johnson, Old Time Schools and School-Books (New York: MacMillan Co., 1904), pp. 54-55.

[4]Ibid., pp. 69-70.

[5]Ibid., pp. 61.

[6]Benjamin Franklin, Proposal Relating to the Education of Youth in Pennsylvania. (Early American Imprints 1639-1800).

[7]Ibid., p. 128.

[8]Ibid., p. 150.

[9]Cordasco, Brief History of Education, p. 122.

[10]The Schools of Providence in 1820 (Report of Committee for revising the school Regulations, June 20, 1820 in Centennial Report, 1899-1900), pp. 42-43.

[11]Horace Mann, The Republic and the School, ed. Lawrence A. Cremin (New York: Teacher's College, Columbia University, 1957), p. 98.

[12]Horace Mann, First Annual Report of the Board of Education (Boston, Dutlons & Wintworth, 1838), pp. 61-62.

[13]Ibid., p. 65.

[14]Carl C. Chandler and Charles H. Gross, ed., The History of American Education Through Readings (Boston: D.C. Heath and Co., 1964), p. 107.

CHAPTER X.   (continued)

[15]Ibid., p. 108.

[16]Ibid.

[17]Ibid., p. 65.

[18]Henry H. Vail, A History of the McGuffey
Readers (Cleveland: Burrow Brothers, Co., 1911),
introduction.

[19]Ibid., p. 10.

[20]Ibid., p. 11.

[21]William H. McGuffey, McGuffey's New Fifth
Eclecic Reader: Selected and Original Exercises for
Schools (New York: Van Antwerp, Bragg and Co., 1866),
pp. 148-149.

[22]Vail, History of McGuffey Reader, p. 4.

[23]McGuffey, McGuffey's Third Eclectic Reader
(New York: American Book Co., 1896), pp. 80-81.

[24]Ibid., p. 81.

[25]Ibid., pp. 31-32.

[26]Vail, History of McGuffey Reader, p. 3.

[27]Ibid., p. 2.

[28]Ibid., p. 2.

CHAPTER XI. JOHN DEWEY AND MORAL EDUCATION

[1]Cordasco, Brief History of Education, p. 139,

[2]Reginald D. Archambault, ed., John Dewey on Education (New York: Random House, 1964), pp. 425-439.

[3]Francis W. Garfurth, ed., John Dewey: Selected Educational Writings (London: Heinemann Educational Books, Ltd., 1966), p. 50.

[4]Archambault, John Dewey on Education, p. 310.

[5]John Dewey, Democracy and Education - An Introduction to the Philosophy of Education (New York: MacMillan Co., 1916), p. 198.

[6]John Dewey, Moral Principles in Education, (New York: Greenwood Press, 1909).

[7]Ibid., p. 49.

[8]Ibid., pp. 22, 23.

[9]Ibid., p. 23.

[10]Ibid., pp. 25, 26.

[11]Ibid., p. 11.

[12]Ibid., p. 14.

[13]Dewey, Democracy & Education, p. 358.

CHAPTER XII.   THE TWENTIETH CENTURY:
SECULARIZATION IN EDUCATION

[1]Character Education, Tenth Yearbook of the Department of Superintendents, (Washington D.C.: National Education Association), 1932.

[2]Cardinal Principles of Secondary Education, Washington D.C. Dept. of the Interior, Bureau of Education, Bulletin #35, 1918.

[3]N.E.A. Bicentennial Idea Book, Washington, D.C. National Education Assembly, 1975.

[4]W. W. Charters, The Teaching of Ideals (New York: The MacMillan Company, 1927).

[5]Hugh Hartshorne & Mark May, Studies in the Instance of Character: Vol. I, Vol. II, Vol. III, (New York: MacMillan, 1928-1930).

[6]Bill Forisha & Barbara Forisha, Moral Development and Education, Professional Educators Publications, (1976).

[7]"Can Schools Teach Ethics?", The Christian Science Monitor, (Dec. 23, 1974), p. 1.

[8]"Moral Education", Newsweek, (March 1, 1976) p. 1.

[9]"George Gallup, 7th Annual Gallup Poll of Public Attitudes Toward Education," reprinted in Phi Delta Kappan, (1975), 57 (4), p. 234.

[10]Nicholas Saunders & Marcia Klafter, The Importance and Desired Characteristics of Moral Education in the Public Schools of the U.S.A.: A Systematic Analysis of Recent Documents, in Russel Hill, & Joan Wallace, Selected Readings in Moral Education, (Philadelphia: Research for Better Schools, Winter, 1976).

CHAPTER XII.   (continued)

[11]Ibid., pp. 14-26.

[12]"She Faces Dismissal," The Herald Journal
(May 12, 1981), p. 2.

[13]D.J. Weeren, Journal of Moral Education,
Vol. 2, No. 1, pp. 35-43.

[14]John Wooden, They Call Me Coach. (New York:
Bantam, 1972).

[15]Dwight Chapin and Jeff Prugh. The Wizard of
Westwood: Coach John Wooden and his UCLA Bruins. New
York: Warner, 1973.

[16]Lawrence Kohlberg, "The Cognitive Developmental
Approach to Socialization," in David Goslin, ed., Hand-
book of Socialization Theory and Research, (Chicago:
Rand McNalley, 1969), pp. 347-480.

[17]Jean Piaget, The Moral Judgement of the Child,
(New York: Free Press, 1965).

[18]Kohlberg, "The Cognitive Developmental Approach
to Socialization," p. 379.

[19]Lawrence Kohlberg Revisions in the theory and
practice of moral development. In W. Damon (ed.) New
Directions for Child Development: Moral Development.
(San Francisco: Jossey Bass, 1978).

[20]Kohlberg, "The Cognitive Developmental Approach
to Socialization," p. 379.

[21]Kenneth Nichols Moral and Ego Development In
Early Adolescents: A Longitudinal Study of Deliberate
Moral and Psychological Education Intervention.   Un-
published doctoral dissertation, 1981.

CHAPTER XII.   (continued)

[22]Lawrence Metcalfe, ed., Values Education: Rationale, Strategies and Procedures, 41st Yearbook, (Washington, D.C.: National Council for the Social Studies, 1971).

[23]James P. Shaver and A. Guy Larkins The Analysis of Public Issues Program (Boston: Houghton Mifflin, 1973.

[24]Louis E. Ruths, Merrill Harmin and Sidney B. Simon, Values and Teaching: Working With Values in the Classroom (Columbus, Ohio: Charles E. Merrill, 1966), p. 37.

[25]Ibid.

[26]Ibid.

APPENDICES

Material in the following appendices is based
on a report listed in Resources in Education obtain-
able from ERIC Document Reproduction Service, (SO 008 489).

APPENDIX A: DIRECT TEACHING

a. Bensley, Marvin L. Coronado Plan: Teacher's
   Guides. San Diego, CA: Pennant, 1974.

b. Blanchette, Zelda Beth, et al. The Human Values
   Series. Austin, TX: Steck-Vaughn, 1970, 1973.

c. Brayer, Herbert O., and Zella W. Cleary. Valuing
   in the Family: A Workshop Guide for Parents.
   San Diego, CA: Pennant, 1972.

d. Character Education Curriculum: Living With Me
   and Others. San Antonio, TX: American Institute
   for Character Education, 1974.

e. Freedom and Responsibility: A Question of Values.
   White Plains, NY: The Center for Humanities, 1973.

f. Hargraves, Richard B. Values: Language Arts.
   Miami FL: Dade County Public Schools, 1971. ED
   064 738.

g. Hawley, Robert C. Human Values in the Classroom:
   Teaching for Personal and Social Growth. Amherst,
   MA: Education Research Associates, 1973.

h. Hillcourt, William. Official Boy Scout Handbook.
   Irving, TX: Boy Scouts of America, 1980.

i. Lakota Woskate: Curriculum Materials Resource
   Unit 6. Spearfish, SD: Black Hills State College,
   1972. ED 066 240.

j. Leondard, Blanche A. Building Better Bridges
   With Ben. Santa Monica, CA: Sunny Enterprises,
   1974.

k. Los Angeles City Schools. The Teaching of Values:
   An Instructional Guide for Kindergarten, Grades
   1-14. Los Angeles, CA: Division of Instructional
   Services, Los Angeles City Schools, 1966.

145

1. Mitsakos, Charles, general ed. The Family of
    Man: A Social Studies Program. Newton, MA:
    Selective Educational Equipment, 1971-74.

m. Pasadena City Schools. Moral And Spiritual
    Values. Pasadena, CA: Division of Instructional
    Services, Pasadena City Schools, 1957.

n. Rucker, W. Ray, et al. Human Values in Education.
    Dubuque, IA: Kendall/Hunt, 1969.

o. Senesh, Lawrence. Our Working World. Chicago,
    IL: Science Research Associates, 1973.

p. Simpson, Bert K. Becoming Aware of Values. San
    Diego, CA: Pennant, 1973.

q. United State History: From Community to Society.
    Teacher's Guide, Grade Six, Project Social Studies.
    Minneapolis, MN: University of Minnesota, 1968.
    ED 068 383.

r. Wooden, John R. They Call Me Coach. New York:
    Bantam Books, 1972.

146

APPENDIX B: MORAL DEVELOPMENT

a. Bender, David, and Gary McCuen. Photo Study
    Cards: Meaning and Values. Anoka, MN: Greenhaven,
    1974.

b. Catalogue of Teaching and Research Materials in
    Moral Education. Vancouver, British Columbia,
    Canada: Association for Values Education and
    Research (A.V.E.R.), University of British
    Columbia, 1975.

c. Fenton, Edwin, ed. Holt Social Studies Curriculum.
    New York, NY: Holt, Rinehart and Winston, 1969-75.
    Includes the following titles: Comparative Political
    Systems, Comparative Economic Systems, The Shaping
    of Western Society, Tradition and Change in Four
    Societies, A New History of the United States,
    The Humanities in Three Cities, and Introduction
    to the Behavioral Sciences.

d. Galbraith, Ronald E., and Thomas M. Jones. Moral
    Reasoning: Teaching Strategies for Adapting Kohlberg
    to the Classroom. Anoka, MN: Greenhaven, (in press).

e. Galbraith, Ronald E., and Thomas M. Jones. "Teach-
    ing Strategies for Moral Dilemmas: An Application
    of Kohlberg's Theory of Moral Development to the
    Social Studies Classroom." Social Education, 39
    (January 1975) pp. 16-22.

f. Hickey, J. "Designing and Implementing a Cor-
    rectional Program Based on Moral Development
    Theory." In Moralization: The Cognitive Develop-
    mental Approach, Lawrence Kohlberg and Elliot
    Turiel, eds. New York, NY: Holt, Rinehart and
    Winston, in press.

g. Kohlberg, Lawrence, and Robert Selman. First
    Things: Values. New York, NY: Guidance Associ-
    ates, 1972. Includes the following titles: The

147

Trouble With Truth, That's No Fair!, You Promised!, But It Isn't Yours . . , and What Do You Do About Rules?

h. Lickonia, Thomas. A Strategy for Teaching Values. New York, NY: Guidance Associates, 1972.

i. Lockwood, Alan. Moral Reasoning: The Value of Life. Columbus, OH: Xerox, 1972.

j. Mattox, Beverly A. Getting It Together: Dilemmas for the Classroom. San Diego, CA: Pennant, 1975.

k. Pagliuso, Susan. A Workbook: Understanding Stages of Development. Toronto, Ontario, Canada: Ontario Institute for Studies in Education, 1975.

l. Piburn, Michael D. "Moral Dilemmas and the Environment." 1973. ED 091 261. Paper presented at the annual meeting of the National Council for the Social Studies, San Francisco, November 19-24, 1974.

m. Porter, Nancy, and Nancy Taylor. How to Assess the Moral Reasoning of Students. Toronto, Ontario, Canada: The Ontario Institute for Studies in Education, 1972.

n. Rules. Boulder, CO: Biological Sciences Curriculum Study, 1974.

o. Selman, Robert L., et al. A Strategy for Teaching Social Reasoning. New York, NY: Guidance Associates, 1974.

p. Selman, Robert L., et al. First Things: Social Reasoning. New York, NY: Guidance Associates, 1974. Series includes the following titles: How Do You Know What Others Will Do:, How Would You Feel?, How Do You Know What's Fair?, and How Can You Work Things Out?

APPENDIX C: ANALYSIS

a. Allender, Donna S., and Jerome S. Allender. I Am the Mayor. Philadelphia, PA: Center for the Study of Federalism, Temple University, 1971.

b. Barr, Robert D. Values and Youth (Teaching Social Studies in an Age of Crisis -No. 2). Washington, D.C.: National Council for the Social Studies, 1971.

c. Bender, David L., and Gary E. McCuen, eds. Opposing Viewpoints Series. Anoka, MN: Greenhaven, 1971-74.

d. Berlak, Harold, and Timothy R. Tomlinson. People/Choices/Decisions. New York, NY: Random House, 1973. Includes the following titles: A Village Family and One City Neighborhood.

e. Brandwein, Paul F. The Social Sciences: Concepts and Values. New York, NY: Harcourt Brace Jovanovich, 1970-75.

f. Brown, Richard, and Van R. Halsey, eds. Amherst Project Units in American History. Menlo Park, CA: Addison-Wesley, 1970-74.

g. Conner, Shirley, et al. Social Studies in the School Program: A Rationale and Related Points of View. Towson, MD: Baltimore County Board of Education, 1970. ED 066 393.

h. Durkin, Mary C., and Anthony H. McNaughton. The Taba Program in Social Science. Menlo Park, CA: Addison-Wesley, 1972-74.

i. Evans, W. Keith, et al. Rational Value Decisions and Value Conflict Resolution: A Handbook for Teachers. Salt Lake City, UT: Granite School District and the Value Analysis Capability Development Programs, University of Utah, 1974.

149

j. Fraenkel, Jack R., series ed. Perspectives in World Order. New York, NY: Random House, 1973, 1975. Includes the following titles: Peacekeeping and The Struggle for Human Rights: A Question of Values.

k. The Good Man, Good Life, and Good Society. Social Studies and Language Arts: 6448.17. Miami, FL: Dade County Public Schools, 1972. ED 073 962.

l. Human Values in an Age of Technology. White Plains, NY: The Center for Humanities, 1972.

m. Law and Justice for Intermediate Grades: Making Value Decisions. New Rochelle, NY: Pathescope Educational Films, 1973.

n. Lippitt, Ronald, Robert Fox, and Lucille Schaible. Social Science Laboratory Units. Chicago, IL: Science Research Associates, 1969.

o. Mehlinger, Howard, and John J. Patrick. American Political Behavior. Lexington, MA: Ginn, 1974.

p. Metcalf, Lawrence E., ed. Values Education: Rationale, Strategies, and Procedures. 41st Yearbook. Washington, D.C.: National Council for the Social Studies, 1971.

q. Meux, Milton, et al. Value Analysis Capability Development Programs: Final Report. Salt Lake City, UT: Granite School District and the Value Analysis Capability Development Programs, University of Utah, 1974.

r. Miller, Harry G., and Samuel M. Vinocur. "A Method for Clarifying Value Statements in the Social Studies Classroom: A Self-Instructional Program." 1972. ED 070 687.

s. Moral Dilemmas of American Presidents: The Agony of Decision. New Rochelle, NY: Pathescope Educational Films, 1974.

t. Nelson, Jack L., series ed. American Values
    Series: Challenges and Choices. Rochelle Park,
    NJ: Hayden, 1974-75.

u. Nelson, Jack L. An Introduction to Value Inquiry:
    A Student Process Book. Rochelle Park, NJ: Hyden,
    1974.

v. Oliver, Donald, and Fred M. Newmann. The Public
    Issues Series. Columbus, OH: Xerox, 1967-74.

w. Origins of American Values: The Puritan Ethic to
    the Jesus Freaks. White Plains, NY: The Center
    for the Humanities, 1973.

x. Payne, Judy R. Introduction to Eastern Philosophy,
    Social Studies: 6414.23. Miami, FL: Dade County
    Public Schools, 1971. ED 071 937.

y. Quigley, Charles N., and Richard P. Longaker.
    Voices for Justice: Role Playing in Democratic
    Procedures. Lexington, MA: Ginn, 1970.

z. Rice, Marion J., and Wilfrid C. Bailey, project
    directors. Political Anthropology: Values, Social-
    ization, Social Control, and Law. Athens, GA:
    Anthropology Curriculum Project, University of
    Georgia, 1968.

aa. Rogers, Vincent R. The Values and Decisions
    Series. Columbus, OH: Xerox, 1972-74.

bb. Ruggiero, Vincent Ryan. The Moral Imperative.
    Port Washington, NY: Alfred Publishing, 1973.

cc. Sayre, Joan. Teaching Moral Values Through Be-
    havior Modification: Intermediate Level. Danville,
    IL: Interstate, 1972.

dd. Sayre, Joan M., and James E. Mack. Teaching Moral
    Values Through Behavior Modification: Primary
    Level. Danville, IL: Interstate, 1973.

151

ee. Shaver, James P., and A. Guy Larkins. _Analysis of Public Issues Program_. Boston, MA: Houghton Mifflin, 1973.

ff. Swenson, William G. _The Search for Values Through Literature: A Practical Teaching Guide_. New York, NY: Bantam, 1973.

gg. Tooni, Linda. _Law and Order: Values in Crisis_. Pleasantville, NY: Warren Schloat, 1971.

hh. Turner, Sheila, ed., and Cornell Capa, series coordinator. _Images of Man I and II_. Englewood Cliffs, NJ: Scholastic, 1972, 1973.

ii. _Values in Mass Communication_. Boston, MA: Allyn and Bacon, 1974.

jj. _Values: Teacher's Edition_. Oakland, CA: Oakland Unified School District, 1972.

kk. Social Studies Methods Texts with Some Emphasis on Value Analysis:

1) Banks, James A. _Teaching Strategies for the Social Studies: Inquiry, Valuing, Decision making_. Reading, MA: Addison-Wesley, 1973.

2) Brubaker, Dale. _Secondary Social Studies for the '70's_. New York, NY: Crowell, 1973.

3) Fraenkel, Jack. _Helping Students Think and Value_. Englewood Cliffs, NJ: Prentice-Hall, 1973.

4) Hunt, Maurice P., and Lawrence E. Metcalf. _Teaching High School Social Studies_. New York, NY: Harper, 1968.

5) Joyce, Bruce P. _New Strategies for Social Education_. Chicago, IL: Science Research Associates, 1972.

6) Massialas, Byron G., and C. Benjamin Cox. _Inquiry in Social Studies_. New York, NY: McGraw-Hill, 1966.

7) Michaelis, John U. <u>Social Studies for Child-</u>
    <u>ren in a Democracy.</u> Englewood Cliffs, NJ:
    Prentice-Hall, 1972.

8) Oliver, Donald, and James Shaver. <u>Teaching</u>
    <u>Public Issues in the High School.</u> Boston, MA:
    Houghton Mifflin, 1966.

9) Smith, Frederick, and C. Benjamin Cox. <u>New</u>
    <u>Strategies and Curriculum in Social Studies.</u>
    Chicago, IL: Rand-McNally, 1969.

10) Taba, Hilda, et al. <u>A Teacher's Handbook to</u>
    <u>Elementary Social Studies: An Inductive Approach.</u>
    Menlo Park, CA: Addison-Wesley, 1971.

APPENDIX D: CLARIFICATION

a. Allen, Rodney F., et al. Deciding How to Live on Spaceship Earth: The Ethics of Environmental Concern. Evanston, IL: McDougal, Littell, 1973.

b. Anderson, Judith L., et al. Focus on Self-Development. Stage One: Awareness; Stage Two: Responding; and Stage Three: Involvement. Chicago, IL: Science Research Associates, 1970, 1971, 1972.

c. Argus Filmstrips. Niles, IL: Argus Communications, 1974.

d. Brandwein, Paul. Self Expression and Conduct: The Humanities. New York, NY: Harcourt Brace Jovanovich, 1974-75.

e. Caprio, Betsy. Poster Ideas for Personalized Learning. Niles, IL: Argus Communications, 1974.

f. Carey, Mauren, et at. Deciding on the Human Use of Power: The Exercise and Control of Power in an Age of Crisis. Evanston, IL: McDougal, Littell, 1974.

g. Casteel, J. Doyle, and Robert J. Stahl. Value Clarification in the Classroom: A Primer. Pacific Palisades, CA: Goodyear, 1975.

h. Casteel, J. Doyle, et al. Valuing Exercises for the Middle School. Gainsville, FL: P.K. Yonge Laboratory School, College of Education, University of Florida, 1974.

i. Church, John G. A Probe into Values. New York, NY: Harcourt Brace Jovanovich, 1973.

j. Clarifying your Values: Guidelines for Living. White Plains, NY: The Center for Humanities, 1974.

k. Cole, Richard. A New Role for Geographic Educa-
    tion: Values and Environmental Concerns. Oak
    Park, IL: National Council for Geographic Educa-
    tion, 1974.

l. Curwin, Richard L., and Gerri Curwin. Developing
    Individual Values in the Classroom. Palo Alto,
    CA: Learning Handbooks, Education Today, 1974.

m. Curwin, Gerri, et al. Dimensions of Personality:
    Search for Values. Dayton, OH: Pflaum, 1972.

n. Deciding Right from Wrong: The Dilemma of
    Morality Today. White Plains, NY: The Center
    for Humanities, 1974.

o. Decision-Making: Dealing with Crises. White
    Plains, NY: The Center for Humanities, 1974.

p. Dinkmeyer, Don. Developing Understanding of
    Self and Others (DUSO), D-1, D-2. Circle Pines,
    MN: American Guidance Service, 1970, 1973.

q. Dunfee, Maxine, and Claudia Crump. Teaching for
    Social Values in the Social Studies. Washington,
    D.C.: Association for Childhood Education Inter-
    national, 1974.

r. Dupont, Henry, et al. Toward Affective Develop-
    ment (TAD). Circle Pines, MN: American Guid-
    ance Service, 1974.

s. Dynamic Consumer Decision Making. New York,
    NY: Educational and Consumer Relations Depart-
    ment, J.C. Penney Company, 1972.

t. Elder, Carl A. Making Value Judgments: Decisions
    for Today. Columbus, OH: Charles E. Merrill,
    1972.

u. Environmental Values Action Cards. St. Paul,
    MN: Minnesota State Department of Education,
    1974.

155

v. Experiences in Decision Making: Elementary Social
    Studies Handbook. Edmonton, Alberta, Canada:
    Alberta Department of Education, 1971.

w. Fischer, Carl, and Walter Limbacher. Dimensions
    of Personality. Dayton, OH: Pflaum, 1969-70,
    1972. Includes the following titles: Let's Begin,
    Now I'm Ready, I Can Do It, What About Me? Here
    I Am, I'm Not Alone, and Becoming Myself.

x. Gelatt, H.B., et al. Deciding. New York, NY:
    College Entrance Examination Board, 1972.

y. Gelatt, H.B., et al. Decisions and Outcomes.
    New York, NY: College Entrance Examination Board,
    1973.

z. Glashagel, Char, and Jerry Glashagel. Valuing
    Families. Akron, OH: Youth Values Project,
    Akron Y.M.C.A., 1974.

aa. Glashgel, Char, and Jerry Glashagel. Valuing
    Youth. Akron, OH: Youth Values Project, Akron
    Y.M.C.A., 1974.

bb. Goodykoontz, William F. Contact. New York, NY:
    Scholastic, 1968-74.

cc. Hall, Brian. Values Clarification as Learning
    Process. Paramus, NJ: Paulist Press, 1973.

dd. Hall, Brain. Valuing: Exploration and Discovery.
    San Diego, CA: Pennant, 1971.

ee. Hanley, Jim, and Don Thompson. Searching for
    Values: A Film Anthology. New York, NY: Learn-
    ing Corporation of America, 1972.

ff. Hard Choices: Strategies for Decision-Making.
    White Plains, NY: The Center for Humanities, 1975.

156

gg. Harmin, Merrill, et al. Clarifying Values Through Subject Matter: Applications for the Classroom. Minneapolis, MN: Winston, 1973.

hh. Harmin, Merrill. Making Sense of Our Lives. Niles, IL: Argus Communications, 1974.

ii. Harmin, Merrill. People Projects. Menlo Park, CA: Addison-Wesley, 1973.

jj. Hawley, Robert C. Value Exploration Through Role Playing: Practical Strategies for Use in the Class room. New York, NY: Hart, 1975.

kk. Hawley, Robert C., et al. Composition for Personal Growth: Values Clarification Through Writing. New York, NY: Hart, 1973.

ll. Howard, Robert, Roles and Relationships: Exploring Attitudes and Values. New York, NY: Westinghouse Learning, 1973.

mm. Howe, Leland W., and Mary Martha Howe. Personalizing Education: Values Clarification and Beyond. New York, NY: Hart, 1975.

nn. Klein, Ronald, et al. Dimensions of Personality: Search for Meaning. Dayton, OH: Pflaum, 1974.

oo. Knapp, Clifford E. "Teaching Environmental Education with a Focus on Values." 1972. ED 070 614.

pp. Kuhn, David J. "Value Education in the Sciences: The Step Beyond Concepts and Processes." 1973. ED 080 317.

qq. Man and His Values. White Plains, NY: Center for the Humanities, 1973.

rr. McPhail, Peter, et al. Lifeline. Niles, IL: Argus Communications, 1975.

ss. McPhail, Peter, et al. Moral Education in the Secondary School. London, England: Longmans, 1972.

157

tt. Miguel, Richard J. Decision: A Values Approach to Decision Making. Columbus, OH: Charles E. Merrill, 1974.

uu. Morrison, Eleanor S., and Mila Underhill Price. Values in Sexuality: A New Approach to Sex Education. New York, NY: Hart, 1974.

vv. The New Model Me. Lakewood, OH: Meeting Modern Problems Project, Lakewood City Public School System, 1973.

ww. O'Fahey, Sheila, et al. Deciding How to Live as Society's Children: Individual Needs and Institutional Expectations. Evanston, IL: McDougal, Littell, 1974.

xx. Paine, Doris M., and Diana Martinez. Guide to Religious Thought: An Examination of Spiritual Value Systems, New York, NY: Bantam, 1974.

yy. Paulson, Wayne. Deciding for Myself: A Values-Clarification Series. Minneapolis, MN: Winston, 1974.

zz. Raths, Louis E. Exploring Moral Values. Pleasantville, NY: Warren Schloat, 1969.

aaa. Raths, Louis E., et al. Values and Teaching: Working with Values in the Classroom. Columbus, OH: Charles E. Merrill, 1966.

bbb. Shaftel, Fannie R., and George Shaftel. Role-Playing for Social Values: Decision Making in the Social Studies. Englewood Cliffs, NJ: Prentice-Hall, 1967.

ccc. Shaftel, Fannie, and George Shaftel. Values in Action. Minneapolis, MN: Winston, 1970.

ddd. Simon, Sidney B. Meeting Yourself Halfway: 31 Value Clarification Strategies for Daily Living. Niles, IL: Argus Communications, 1974.

eee. Simon, Sidney B., and Jay Clark. More Values Clarification: A Guidebood for the Use of Values Clarification in the Classroom. San Diego, CA: Pennant, 1975.

fff. Simon, Sidney B., and Howard Kirschenbaum, eds. Readings in Values Clarification. Minneapolis, MN: Winston, 1973.

ggg. Simon, Sidney B., et al. Values Clarification: A Handbook of Practical Strategies for Teachers and Students. New York, NY: Hart, 1972.

hhh. Smith, M.F. The Valuing Approach to Career Education. Waco, TX: Education Achievement Corporation, 1973-74.

iii. Values Series. Santa Monica, CA: BFA Educational Media, 1972.

jjj. Waltz, Garry R., ed. Communique: Resources for Practicing Counselors. 2(May 1973). Ann Arbor, MI: ERIC/CAPS, School of Education, University of Michigan. ED 075 766.

kkk. Williams, Elmer. Values and the Valuing Process: Social Studies for the Elementary School, Proficiency Module #5. Athens, GA: Department of Elementary Education, University of Georgia, 1972. ED 073 990.

lll. Wrenn, C. Gilbert, and Shirley Schwarzrock. Coping With Series. Circle Pines, MN: American Guidance Service, 1973.

mmm. Y Circulator, 4(Spring 1973). New York, NY: National Council of YMCAs. ED 080 403.

ABOUT THE AUTHORS

Larry C. Jensen is a professor of psychology at Brigham Young University who specializes in moral development and the psychology of the family. He has written numerous books and articles including: What's Right? What's Wrong? A Psychological Analysis of Moral Behavior Washington, D.C. Public Affairs Press, 1975, and Responsibility and Morality: Helping Children Become Responsible and Morally Mature Provo, Utah: Brigham Young University Press, 1979, and Moral Reasoning U. of Nebraska Press, 1978. He has developed and teaches a course entitled Moral Development in the Family.

Richard S. Knight is an associate professor of secondary education who is a social studies specialist. He is a former high school psychology and economics teacher and was a social worker in Los Angeles. He has written Students' Rights: Issues In Constitutional Freedoms Boston: Houghton Mifflin, 1973, and Interdisciplinary Curriculum Strand: Values Education with Eyre Turner, Salt Lake City: Utah State Office of Education, 1980.

He has developed and teaches a course entitled Value Education.